Country Houses Today

Published in Great Britain in 2006 by John Wiley & Sons Ltd

Copyright © 2006

John Wiley & Sons Ltd, The Atrium, Southern Gate, Chichester,
West Sussex, PO19 8SQ, England
telephone +44 (0)1243 779 777

Email (for orders and customer service enquires): cs-books@wiley.co.uk
Visit our Home Page on www.wiley.co.uk or www.wiley.com

Other Wiley Editorial Offices

John Wiley & Sons Inc., 111 River Street, Hoboken, NJ 07030, USA

Jossey-Bass, 989 Market Street, San Francisco, CA 94103-1741, USA

Wiley-VCH Verlag GmbH, Boschstr. 12, D-69469 Weinheim, Germany

John Wiley & Sons Australia Ltd, 42 McDougall Street, Milton,
    Queensland 4064, Australia

John Wiley & Sons (Asia) Pte Ltd, 2 Clementi Loop #02-01
    Jin Xing Distripark, Singapore 129809

John Wiley & Sons Canada Ltd, 5353 Dundas Street West, Suite 400,
    Etobicoke, Ontario, Canada M9B 6H8

Wiley also publishes its books in a variety of electronic formats. Some
content that appears in print may not be available in electronic books.

ISBN-13 978 047 01647 3
ISBN-10 0 470 01647 7

Cover Photograph © Eduard Hueber/archphoto
Cover design by Artmedia Press Ltd, UK

Page design and layouts by Ian Lambot Studio
Picture research by Beatrice Galilee
Printed and bound by Conti Tipocolor, Italy

Country Houses Today

Jeremy Melvin

Series Designer Liz Sephton

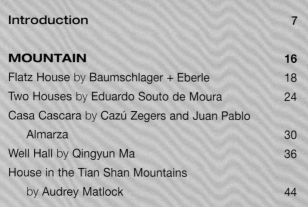

contents

Executive Commissioning Editor: Helen Castle
Content Editor: Louise Porter
Publishing Assistant: Calver Lezama

Any book about contemporary country houses has to face two more or less immutable conditions. One is that new country houses in the traditional sense of being the economic, social and symbolic hub of a great and lucrative estate are extremely rare; now almost all new houses in the countryside are just that – rural retreats or residences that are not economically dependent on land. There are none of the traditional type in this book, and only one example was commissioned by a member of the old European aristocracy – and that, ironically, is in Sweden, a country where Social Democracy has held sway for nearly a century and the aristocracy were never as rich as their counterparts in France or Britain.

Introduction

The other condition, rather more mutable, is that these 'houses in the country' are, as Arts and Crafts architects found at the turn of the nineteenth and twentieth centuries and FRS Yorke argued in his book *The Modern House*, first published in 1934, ideal laboratories for innovative design; statutory planning controls permitting, those who commission and design them are free to engage in architectural experiment, and if they seek to express stasis and stability, it is by choice rather than obligation or expectation. So to fly in the face of semantics and the scholarship which underpins it, the country house today is more likely to be a rural retreat of avant-garde design than a device that uses traditional conventions to express power; shorn of the intimate connection to the land and community of a semi-feudal demesne, its architectural references and audiences can just as well be international as local. Individual examples may well have to address specific issues, such as the notoriously stringent statutory planning controls in the UK, but a measure of their significance is that the proviso that

Anthony Salvin and William Burn, Harlaxton Manor, Grantham, Lincolnshire, 1837.
Harlaxton Manor is testimony to the sheer joy of country house building. Its client, Gregory Gregory, had no direct heir and disliked his cousin on whom the estate was entailed, but still experimented with various architects to create one of the most extraordinary buildings in the English country house tradition.

was meant to usher in a generation of new country houses by permitting examples of outstanding design quality has hardly produced an avalanche of innovative design.

Together, these two conditions render obsolete the question of whether the country house would survive the issue, which ran through any study of the subject in the couple of generations following the Second World War. Naturally, the focus was on the fate of the great and historic examples that damp, death duties, dry rot and general decrepitude had brought to the point of despair. It prompted a revival of interest in the subject, and works like Mark Girouard's *Life in the English Country House* helped to create an understanding of the social and architectural context of traditional country houses. What they could not foresee was that the ranks of the wealthy would continue to expand, more quickly, perhaps, than ever before. But their wealth would not find its way into land; political influence could be bought in other and generally cheaper ways. However, people still build houses in the country, and they are the subject of this book.

This introduction attempts to outline some architectural characteristics of the country house today, and indicate how they might have evolved. It suggests that globalisation's strange and complex effects on country houses may lead initially to an apparent paradox, but that itself mutates into a changed relationship between house and landscape that certain sorts of design idiom, largely derived from Modernism and whose virtues are more evident in light of globalisation, are uniquely able to explore and exploit. That is why the houses in this book are divided not by style or location, but by the overriding physical conditions of the site and its surroundings.

Globalisation is as much an influence on country houses as it is on any aspect of contemporary architecture, but its particular manifestations here take several strange and complex forms. The sort of people who have the means and inclination to build country houses today are very likely to have derived some benefit from, and could well play a more active role in, one or more aspects of globalisation. They may travel extensively; they might be involved with the rapid movement of vast and invisible quantities of money or information. They are almost certain to be familiar with patterns of change, transience and impermanence. These conditions could seem to be at odds with the values that country houses customarily exude – of solidity, permanence and the endurance of a particular social order – but this clash is less of a paradox than a particular variant on a common theme throughout the history of country houses. Under the guise of stasis, new country houses very often marked the ascent of a new family into the ruling oligarchy. Architecture was the means to resolve this paradox, and their overall architectural aims are neatly encapsulated in the sentiments expressed by the impetuous young Prince Tancredi Falconeri in *The Leopard*, Giuseppe di Lampedusa's great dissection of the vicissitudes of aristocratic privilege, when he says to his uncle Fabrizio, Prince of Salina: "Things must change if they are to stay the same."

Architecture has always been able to cope with the paradox of instituting change in order to allow things to stay the same. What made traditional country houses especially effective at this was that their

Mark Girouard, *Life in the English Country House*, Yale University Press (London), 1978.
Girouard's book was pivotal in creating an interest in the plight of the traditional English country house that by the middle of the twentieth century was in peril, threatened equally by the expense of their upkeep and the demise of the landed classes.

James Paine, New Wardour Castle, Wiltshire, 1770-6. Vast and slightly austere, New Wardour Castle belongs to the English Palladian tradition which dominated country house building during the eighteenth century. Like its companions, its classical design seems to exude an effortless dominion over nature, just as its occupants expected to exude endless dominion over their fellow humans. Built for a family of recusant Catholics, Wardour's political and economic implications are formidably complicated.

architecture gave aesthetic expression to specific social beliefs, particularly the assumption that land, wealth and political power went hand-in-hand. There were always alternative sources of wealth and, by the nineteenth century, particularly in Britain, country house architects were increasingly projecting a fiction as industrialisation and commerce increasingly outstripped land as the principal source of economic power. But the connection between political power and country houses endured: it motivated the Elizabethan magnates who bankrupted themselves to impress their queen, and even someone as enigmatic as the childless builder of Harlaxton Manor, Gregory Gregory, who might have hoped in the 1830s that his new house would catch the eye of the king and lead to a peerage. As recently as the 1920s, that belief was strong enough to persuade Arthur Lee to donate his own country house, Chequers, to the nation for the use of Prime Ministers who could no longer be relied upon to have one of their own.

If the relationship between power, land and country houses started to creak in the nineteenth century, it has now finally collapsed. Anthony Sampson, an acute analyst of power structures, documents the decline of land – unless it happens to have part of London's West End on it – as a standard of wealth in *Who Runs This Place?* Although, he concedes, two great rural landowning magnates made it onto *The Sunday Times* list of Britain's richest people in 2003, their art collections were more valuable than their hundreds of thousands of acres. The alternative and now far more effective sources of wealth that catapult people into the highest places on the list may take advantage of global communications and flows of goods, services and capital, but they are doing no more than fulfilling the nature of money that Georg Simmel described in *The Philosophy of Money* in the early twentieth century.

Chequers Court, Buckinghamshire, an original twelfth-century house restored and enlarged by John Hawtrey in 1565. The official country residence of the British Prime Minister, Chequers was donated to the nation by Arthur Lee (1868-1947) under the Chequers Estate Act of 1917. Lee, who was also the 1st Viscount Lee of Fareham, was married to an American heiress and was a Member of Parliament. His gift recognised the onset of a new political era in which Prime Ministers could no longer be counted upon to be drawn from the landed classes and thus equipped with their own country houses.

The relative decline of land in value is one reason for its decline as a source of political power, but other alternatives have also emerged. As journalist John Lloyd has observed, the media has an unaccountable influence over politics. One newspaper or television station could exert more influence than any amount of agricultural land, and all one needs to obtain a peerage, if recent allegations are true, is to make a loan to a political party of a quantity that, if turned into a construction project, would barely make an impact. All this merely bears out what Alfred Harmsworth satirised when he said, "If I want a peerage, I'll buy one like an honest man," but as Britain's leading press magnate in the early twentieth century he did not even need to get his cheque book out to become first Baron and later Viscount Northcliffe.

So it is nothing new for the architecture of country houses to address the conditions of change and fluidity. What has changed, in view of the collapse of this old relationship between power, land and country houses, is how the examples in this book make those conditions explicit; doing so now is less a paradoxical contrast between expressions of stasis and impermanence than of the mutation of tradition. Traditional country houses appropriated and merged historical motifs, sometimes with extraordinary skill and invention, and occasionally with highly sophisticated planning, to reimpose stability.

If the effect of what we now call globalisation first undermined and then destroyed the troika of land, power and architecture that traditional country houses represent, it has also opened up new possibilities for the design of contemporary examples. Many of the examples in this book consciously strive to create a new imagery, sometimes from positions established in other areas of contemporary design or visual culture; sometimes from an explicit relationship with, or appreciation of, the peculiarities of the site. On occasion a house springs from a combination of the two. But there are numerous and quite distinct aspects to the architectural possibilities, which recent political and economic change has brought into being.

The first is geographical. Only a few years ago the idea that there would be worthwhile examples of country house architecture emanating from China, the former Soviet republics and the Communist bloc would have been unthinkable. Of course, the emergence of a monied class that can afford to build rural retreats is a logical product of the political changes and economic developments that have swept through those countries, but coming at a particular moment not just in their own national evolution but also of international change, quite how such architecture has emerged has a particular, contingent twist. The architecture of these houses naturally reflects wider architectural trends. While in Poland, Russia, Kazakhstan and China, elephantine augmentations of traditional design – usually with the latest modern technology bolted on – predominate in architectural production, three of those countries, at least, have a small but significant avant-garde that is trying to assimilate local, regional and national building conditions within an international intellectual culture. The three houses in Russia, China and Poland bring this merger into the specific context of domestic architecture, where it becomes part of the means by which this new class is defining its own identity, and in this sense international ideas carry a premium.

The fourth of these houses, in Kazakhstan, shows how the possibilities of country house architecture are spreading to places where they were previously socially, politically or technically impossible. Each of the first three countries has a tradition of rural homes – albeit quite different in style – but many Kazakhs went straight from nomadism to urban living, a dramatic change effected under a regime that was not exactly favourable towards private country house building. Although there is little tradition of rural domestic architecture, there is, at least in the area of the country where this

World map showing the locations of the houses included in this book. The geographical picture that emerges from this book is very different to how it would have been only a decade ago. Even in the late 1990s, the idea that there would be worthwhile examples of country houses emerging in China, the former Soviet republics and elsewhere in the Communist bloc would have been unthinkable.

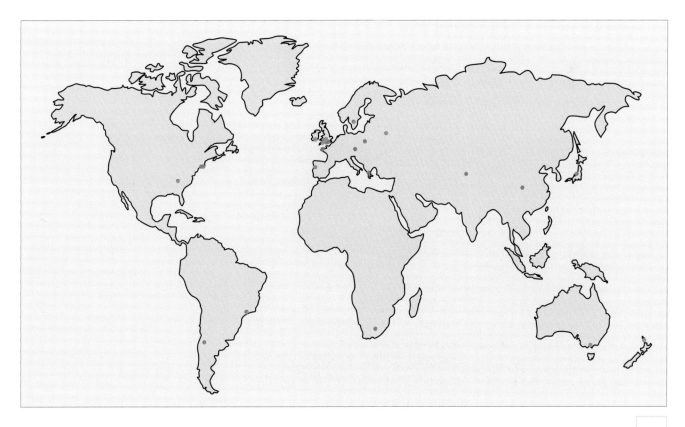

house is located, some of the world's most spectacular scenery – but given the ground conditions, scenery which can only be made habitable by modern engineering expertise. The clients, a Kazakh businessman with interests in various parts of the world and his wife, expressly sought to match contemporary technology with contemporary imagery, but it is an imagery and a lifestyle that cannot avoid being influenced by the landscape.

This house is an extreme case of a common theme which runs through many of the examples in this book. Its origins come from many directions. At the end of the eighteenth century the Romantic Movement opened the door to a different appreciation of nature: no longer would intellectuals travelling across the Alps do as Winckelmann did, and lower the blinds to avoid having to look at the wilds of nature. Buoyed by the nascent discipline of aesthetics, which Terry Eagleton argues both acknowledged the power of emotions that came from sensory experience, but also sublimated them to the reason of a philosophical discourse, new ways of looking started to emerge. And along came Turner, Caspar David Friedrich and Ruskin, while at the Glienicke Park outside Berlin, Karl Friedrich Schinkel and the landscape designer Peter Lenné turned the balance between nature and nurture into an allegory of the relationship between Germany and Italy or the Gothic and classical worlds, and a symbolic journey between them. Such aesthetic theory added a new and more subtle dimension to the relationship between land, power and architecture by introducing the possibility of ideological manipulation. That may initially have helped to reinforce that trinity, but by opening the whole issue of appearance and meaning, ultimately paved the way for different aesthetic experiences that would question it. Paradoxically, the whole panoply of aesthetic theory made it possible to appreciate a view as just a view: not for the power that came with it, the dominion it implied over other souls, or the wealth that it generated.

The Picturesque Movement certainly recognised the range of effect that landscape design could evoke. Under its influence, natural features were manipulated, shaped and placed to maximise their scenic qualities. It took some time for these visual principles to find their way into the architecture of

Glienicke Park, Berlin, 1826. As designed by Karl Friedrich Schinkel and landscape architect Peter Lenné, Glienicke Park stood as an allegory of the relationship between the Gothic and classical worlds, and a symbolic journey between them.

Mackay Hugh Baillie Scott, Blackwell, Lake Windemere, Westmoreland (now Cumbria), **1898-9.** With its roughcast render walls, sandstone window surrounds and mullions, Cumbrian green slate roof and traditional Lakeland chimneys, Blackwell is conscientiously vernacular. An Arts and Crafts house *par excellence*, it featured prominently in Herman Muthesius's *Das Englische Haus*, Berlin, 1904.

the buildings from which these vistas were seen, but at Luscombe Castle in Devon (1800), Nash and Repton came close to producing the sort of effect that the houses in this book achieve. Its owner, a member of the Hoare family of bankers, had the means to engage with the landscape aesthetically rather than economically or socially, and by adopting the Gothic style, Nash had the freedom to create angled and variable views towards features in the park. Though scenery is as much a product of human artifice as the architecture, such designs introduce the idea of a different relationship between landscape and building, based on aesthetics rather than politics.

Ruskin would later lend all his rhetorical force to the idea that Gothic architecture was the only medium that could bring humans closer to nature and the divine order which he believed underlay it. When that assumption collapsed with the recognition, following Darwin, that nature was rather more complicated than Ruskin assumed, architects and architectural theorists pursued other directions. One line of enquiry developed another line of Ruskinian thought, marrying his doctrine of truth to materials with his view that individual workers should have freedom to express themselves in their work. Such ideas informed Philip Webb and Richard Norman Shaw, two consummate country house architects of the late nineteenth century, and

their pupils who helped to fashion the Arts and Crafts Movement. Their
commissions were often classic houses in the country: large but not
enormous homes for wealthy industrialists or successful professionals
surrounded by just enough land to give privacy, but not too much to drain
capital from more profitable business ventures. And if their social
ramifications were less overtly ambitious than those of a traditional country
house, the claims that some Arts and Crafts architects made for architecture's
ability to heal social ills through overcoming the division of labour were as
grandiose as they were ludicrous.

Ultimately, the relationship that each of these houses develops with its
immediate landscape owes more to the Romantic Movement than to the
traditional notion of the country house, based on the triad of power, wealth
and land. But none of them is recognisably Gothic, and only one classical in
the strict sense. Instead, the majority appropriate some derivation of
Modernism to develop particular relationships with their setting. The aesthetic
result tends to come in two separate but related parts. One is the physical

form and appearance of the house itself, which may or may not relate to other examples of the architect's oeuvre or broader currents in contemporary architecture. The other is how the design constructs a way of viewing nature, but part of the delight of these houses is in relating a way of looking with the aesthetics of appearance. In this rarified sense, form and function merge.

Between them these houses also cover a wide spectrum of the way architecture can relate to nature. In the four sections devoted to elemental landscape forms – mountain, forest, ocean and plain – those relationships vary from obvious and direct to tentative and tantalising, but each of the houses adopts a sophisticated aesthetic strategy to construct it, underpinned by modern technology, materials and engineering. It is this combination which allows the relationships to become in some cases almost visceral, such as the dialogue between orthogonal forms, a steep slope and a distant view that Eduardo Souto de Moura creates, or the ethereal balance between interior and exterior in Kengo Kuma's Forest Floor House. Both draw on other artistic or architectural traditions – Souto de Moura on Minimalist art; Kuma on traditional Japanese architecture and its reinterpretation by such Modernist masters as Bruno Taut, but those traditions alone do not account for the unique architectural synthesis of observing and appearance that each creates.

It is relationships of these sorts that characterise country houses today, and which explain the division into generic landscape features. Through these varied contemporary, sophisticated and, in some cases, technology-dependent approaches to architecture, people who negotiate and exploit the vicissitudes of contemporary urbanised and globalised life can appreciate natural wonders, be they mountains, forests, oceans or plains. The fifth category is also about a direct and visceral relationship to landscape, but in this case it is land that has been worked and reworked by human endeavour to become a cultural artefact in its own right. It is not quite as different from the other categories as it might superficially appear; where they condense their human intervention into the fabric of the houses themselves, in the Narrative Landscape human activity is stretched across a wider territory and, generally, a much longer period of time. The narratives can be real, such as the precinct around Old Wardour Castle, which inscribes 600 years of country house history within a few square miles, or they can be sophisticatedly fictitious, as at Sphinx Hill, where the presence of the Thames helps to anchor an iconography of house and garden.

Finally, narrative can be transformative, as at the Lower Mill Estate outside Cirencester. As a former gravel pit it counts, in English planning parlance, as a brownfield or recycled industrial land site, but no obvious trace of gravel extraction remains. Its scarred landscape makes a tabula rasa for numerous leading architects to imagine what a rural house could be like, without the obligations of maintaining an estate, parish church, school and pack of hounds, where technology could control a global business empire and where travel is as likely to be by helicopter as by car. Yet what connects such a vision to the dreams of the Elizabethans, the Palladians or even the nineteenth-century neo-Goths is a sense that design brings pleasure. What endures is not political ambition or social obligation, but the possibilities of architecture, in all its varied guises.

John Outram, Sphinx Hill, Oxfordshire, 2003.
John Outram's design for Sphinx Hill combines the idea of a country house as a place of intellectual pleasures as well as relaxation.

MOUNTAIN

Flatz House

Baumschlager & Eberle
Schaan, Liechtenstein 2000

A bold volumetric concrete composition in front of a scarred and ancient mountain range, this house deliberately enters into a dialogue with one of the archetypal elements of landscape. Through this characteristic it transcends its immediate surroundings and so, despite its suburban setting, it becomes a country house. In general, Baumschlager & Eberle's work contrasts the power of abstract forms with delicately layered planes and surfaces, which draw out the tactile quality of their materials. Here they bring their penchant for abstraction and boldness to the fore precisely because of the drama of the backdrop and banality of the neighbourhood. The raw, shuttered-concrete surfaces might even echo the engineering structures that make mountainous regions habitable – the bridges and dams, for instance – rather than the conventional domestic architecture of such areas where the ubiquitous oversailing roofs jettison the snow and shelter the winter fuel. Although the house is situated in the tiny Duchy of Liechtenstein, the architects are Austrian, and are active participants in the sense that contemporary Austrian architects have turned to abstraction as a way of recapturing a national architectural identity. This building seems to engage in something more serious and certainly more mysterious than anything in the vernacular tradition. Home to a doctor's family with five children, it has to provide them with the accommodation they require, but also transport them through imaginative design from their surroundings to the lofty realm of Alpine peaks.

Baumschlager & Eberle's strategy for achieving this aim is sophisticated and multi-faceted. The first and most obvious move is to give the house a bunker-like exterior to the road. Its only opening at ground level is a darkly uninviting garage. Next to it are a guest room and study with no prospect other than a small enclosed courtyard, though these are concealed behind the front wall. The route towards the front door runs outside the building itself, against a flank wall. But these architects are too sensitive to domesticity to allow the impression of solidity to remain unqualified. Even from the street various openings, including a horizontal slot in the front wall, suggest that this building is not mute. As the path rises alongside the garage, the complexity of the composition starts to reveal itself, and although the house is still at this point more austere than inviting, it is clear it is no concrete bunker. The long cantilever of the first floor confirms this subtlety of expression; it implies a sense of detachment from the ground and upward movement to the mountain peaks, symbolically translating the quotidian experience of walking up the garden path into an almost spiritual occasion.

At the top a shorter cantilever serves as a porch and shades a glass wall which reveals something of the interior. What from below seemed an

Opposite: **Flatz House, Schaan, Liechtenstein.** View from west. A bold and angular composition in maize-coloured concrete, the contrast with the jagged and striated mountains diverts attention from the immediate setting in its dialogue between an elemental landscape feature and archetypal geometrical forms.

Below: **Flatz House, Schaan, Liechtenstein.**
Basement: apparently impenetrable from the street apart from the garage's dark maw, it also contains a two-room apartment around a small, private courtyard

Below: **Flatz House, Schaan, Liechtenstein.**
Ground floor: having ascended the narrow, stepped path, the house's compositional effects begin to reveal themselves: a small garden and pool in the angle of the L-shaped plan which faces south and west. Windows, views and staircases delineate the internal space into zones for a kitchen, dining, study and long living room

Below: **Flatz House, Schaan, Liechtenstein.**
First floor: the interlocking cuboid shapes give this floor the smallest internal space, but provide a generous, sheltered and private terrace off the parents' bedroom

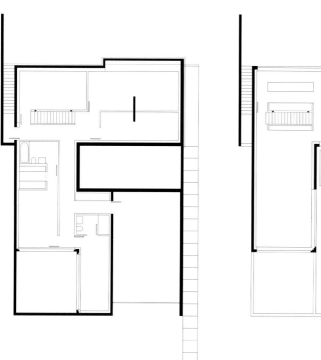

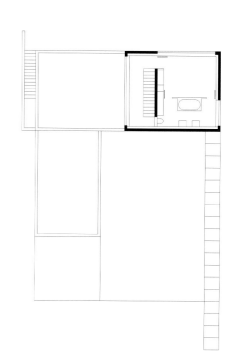

Left: **Flatz House, Schaan, Liechtenstein.** The house has an angular permanence against the constantly shifting skies and seasonally changing mountains. Its design deliberately stresses relationships to these natural elements to lift it above the suburban qualities of its immediate setting

Right: **Flatz House, Schaan, Liechtenstein.**
Internal angle in the ground-floor garden. The
formal composition and the position of the
windows creates an interplay between restricted
views into enclosed spaces which belong to the
architectural composition, and the longer views
which reach to nature – as far the the Swiss
mountains and the Rhine Valley

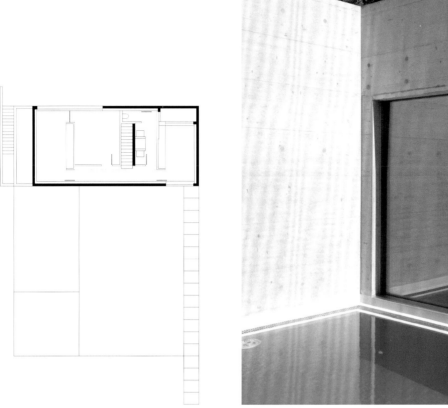

Above: **Flatz House, Schaan, Liechtenstein.**
Second floor: three bedrooms for children – note
how the right hand one has two windows, one
with a restricted view onto a tiny courtyard, the
other outwards across the landscape

impenetrable volume now invites entry as the harshness of the concrete surface yields to smoothly transparent glass, although the main spaces remain hidden behind an internal wall. A neat balance is effected between appearing inviting yet retaining a sense of privacy. Behind this wall is the main living area: a dining room, kitchen and living room, arranged in an L-shape so that the spaces can flow into each other but still retain their own definition. Carefully contrived but restricted views link the spaces and look out across the swimming pool and lawn in the angle of the L. Though the kitchen and living room have large windows these overlook the immediate garden, making intimate and domestic activities such as swimming, cooking and eating the focus of this floor. The interiors are light and airy, with enough wood in the finishes to give them a degree of warmth and arranged so as to construct a series of visual relationships between them as a way of humanising what, from the road, had appeared a forbidding and closed shape.

On the two upper floors this strategy takes on a different dimension. Here, floor to ceiling windows offer dramatic but carefully controlled views of the distant mountains. These spaces are bedrooms, a principal suite on the first floor leading to a terrace sheltered by the cantilever and with three children's rooms on the top floor. Rather than focus on the immediate relationships linking siblings, parents and children, these spaces are private and each fashions its own intimacy with the mountains. It is a visual way of differentiating between the various individuals within the family as well as making them aware of what lies beyond the family's immediate limits, but the frames of the windows still control the view.

Like much of Baumschlager & Eberle's work, this house first establishes a relationship with nature through contrast: the confrontation between regular, cuboid forms and the organic shapes of landscape. But they are too subtle to leave their designs as generic oppositions between nature and artifice. Though the basic volumes of their designs are often regular, they are arranged so as to introduce layers of complexity and surprise that sometimes approach the surreal, such as the precariously long top-floor cantilever. Heightening the abstraction of the architecture has the effect of reinforcing its contrast with natural forms. Then they interweave further contrasting relationships, often by juxtaposing different materials, as here where rough, impermeable concrete is partnered by smoothly transparent glass, consciously playing with their inherent, architectonic characteristics.

Nature, form and materials are the most basic elements of architecture and can remain purely abstract. Baumschlager & Eberle make them specific and contingent by infusing them with functional requirements and specific reactions to the site. It is this principle, for example, that determines the overhang of the first floor above the front door, meeting the functional need for shelter immediately above the entrance without introducing a porch which would undermine the purity of the formal composition. Through experience, familiarity and use the apparent abstractions of the design become logical and even legible.

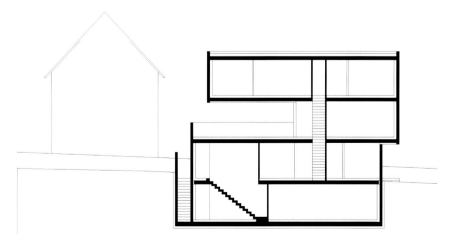

Left: **Flatz House, Schaan, Liechtenstein.**
A north-south section through the house, looking east with north on the left

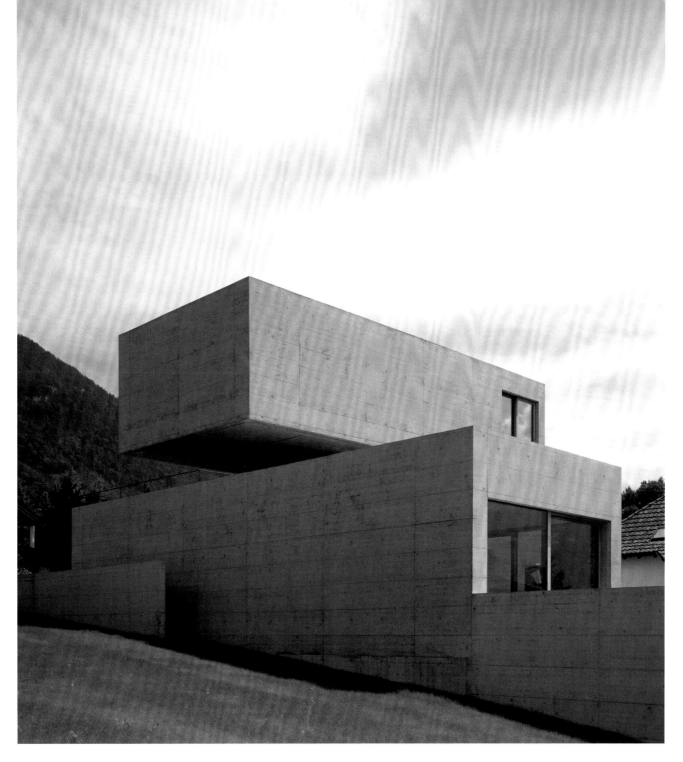

Above: **Flatz House, Schaan, Liechtenstein.**
View from the north-west – until entered the house
is minimal and enigmatic

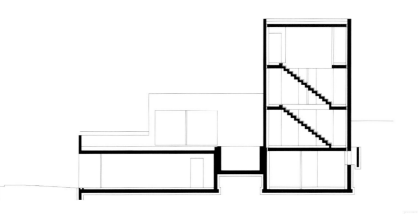

Right: **Flatz House, Schaan, Liechtenstein.**
West-east section looking north

Two Houses

Eduardo Souto de Moura

Ponte de Lima, Portugal   2002

A steeply sloping site is the essence of building in mountainous landscapes. In this relatively modest pair of houses in Ponte de Lima, some way to the north of his home city of Oporto in Portugal, Eduardo Souto de Moura takes the opportunity to explore two distinct ways of living on a gradient. The houses are similarly sized rectilinear boxes, but while one cantilevers horizontally away from the hill, the other follows its slope. Though ensuring that they fit into the same overall conception, that simple move makes the houses about as different as any pair of the same size and form, and sharing the same site, could be.

Souto de Moura has proved himself a master of pairing elemental landscape forms with refined artificial objects. His football stadium at Braga,

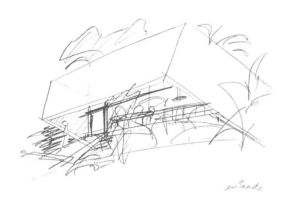
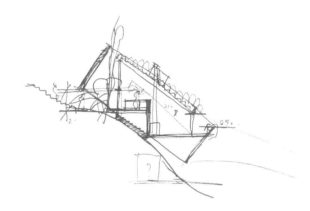

not far from these houses, inserts one of its grandstands into a gaping hole in a mountainside left by a quarry, from where it emerges as if in a fierce struggle – reminiscent of Michaelangelo's unfinished *Dying Slaves* who strive to complete their death throes before yielding to petrified eternity – to achieve refinement and satisfy purpose. Meanwhile, lacking such a dialectic, the other grandstand's flamboyant wing-like structural devices to its rear provide the support which its twin takes from the living rock.

The mountainous and picturesque province of Minho, where these houses are situated, embodies the power and architectural potential of the landscape that helped to mould the particular school of contemporary Portuguese architecture initiated by Fernando Tavora and brought to fruition by Alvaro Siza. Alongside this appreciation of setting, they recognised the qualities of the Portuguese vernacular tradition, whose forms can seem to be simple refinements of natural shapes, their status as buildings rather than nature marked by colouring them white to stand out in the sun against the clear blue skies. To this they added an increasing awareness of broader and

Above: **Two Houses, Ponte de Lima, Portugal.** Souto de Moura explored the spatial possibilities of contrasting angles of similarly sized cuboids in numerous sketches

Above: **Two Houses, Ponte de Lima, Portugal.**
"No meaning if separated": the different positions of similar objects, such as the swimming pools and the different angles of the main forms, are all part of a unified ensemble

more sophisticated architectural traditions, Siza in particular absorbing Alvar Aalto's influence and, from the 1970s, beginning to work abroad. Even before Souto de Moura started his own practice in 1980 after some time in Siza's studio, these influences had begun to coalesce into a recognisable regional adaptation of Modernism, where forms that appear to be simple and straightforward reveal themselves, on examination, to be anything but. Windows might occur in irregular places, or corners which had seemed to be right angles may be obtuse, acute, or even curved. Often drawing attention to some aspect of the site or responding to a functional condition, these departures from expectation make the forms expressive rather than banal and repetitive. Souto de Moura has a personal interest in artists such as Donald Judd, the master of Minimalist expression who explored the territory between repetition and difference to great effect.

These modest houses, designed as two family homes, illustrate this aspect of Souto de Moura's work. Placing them at different angles immediately challenges their similar forms and functions, and their structure

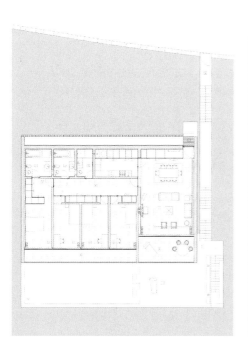 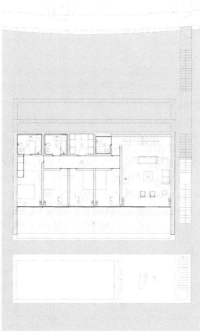

Above: Two Houses, Ponte de Lima, Portugal.
Though the views are similar, they are framed
differently

Left: Two Houses, Ponte de Lima, Portugal.
Plans of the two houses, horizontally cantilevered
(far left) and sloping *(left)*. In the horizontal house,
all accommodation is on the same level. In the
sloping house bedrooms and a double-height
living room are on the lower level *(illustrated)*,
with the kitchen and dining area on the upper,
entrance level

Right: **Two Houses, Ponte de Lima, Portugal.**
Site plan

Below: **Two Houses, Ponte de Lima, Portugal.**
Section through the horizontal house, inspired in
part by an elegantly angled bottle holder

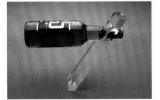

puts considerable demands on contemporary engineering. It is not easy to project a floor from the hillside, nor to maintain the equipoise of a box on so steep a slope. On its own, either house would set up a particular and potentially absorbing relationship with its mountain setting, but the deliberate contrast between the two adds an extra and dynamic dimension. The contrast is what interests Souto de Moura, who writes that the two houses would have "no meaning if separated". The duality immediately suggests the first principle of Modernist uncertainty, namely that there is no single correct solution, and then stretches contemporary engineering to prove it. Souto de Moura is not interested in abstractions for their own sake, but rather in the way they interact with particular conditions to create a tangible entity, a realised object which through its connections to abstraction and references to broader architectural ideas has a significance beyond itself.

Viewed as sculptural objects, these houses would have a certain fascination, but what makes them architectural, and weaves more layers of meaning into them, is the manner in which their programmatic requirements have been met. Both have identical accommodation on similar floor areas: parents' and three children's bedrooms, a couple of bathrooms, kitchen, dining and living areas, as well as a swimming pool. One house places this all

on the same level. An entrance on the corner leads straight into a large living room, combining dining and sitting areas. Off it is a kitchen and door to the bedroom corridor. But straight ahead from the entrance and framed by the insistent dimensions of the living room is a spectacular view of a tree-covered ridge just out of reach, and distant mountain peaks. To move through the living room and out onto the delicately poised balcony and observation platform beyond is to become detached from the ground as it falls away below. In this house the bedrooms too seem to detach themselves into a concentrated, almost coenobitic relationship with the view, a point made explicit by placing the children's desks by the windows. The wet rooms are more earthbound and logically placed against the slope where it adjoins the house.

In the second house the immediate presence of the ground, as opposed to the distant presence of a view, is the strongest impression. The entrance to this house is just off its centre and also straight into a dining area that adjoins a kitchen. But the relationship between accommodation and slope is immediately apparent, because the double-height living room reaches to this level, and stairs lead straight down to it. There is no avoiding the presence of the slope. Again a corridor to the bedrooms leads off the living room, and all the main spaces face onto a balcony or terrace, but the view is lower, less distant and framed by two side walls and a front wall which betray the diagonal of the hillside.

Souto de Moura describes the contrast between the two houses thus: one is "enveloped by the landscape … levelling, imminent"; the other "looks high, distant … to the mountain". This contrast depends on the two approaches to a given site, which between them highlight different qualities in it. They also refer to alternative strands of architectural tradition, and the deep cultural resonance of combined shelter and prospect. Yet the overall design for the two houses separates and reassembles that combination, weaving a consciously intellectual, historically aware influence into an otherwise elemental relationship.

Souto de Moura's teacher Fernando Tavora used to say, around the time Venturi coined 'both/and' as a contrast to 'either/or', the more elusive phrase "in architecture, the opposite is also true". In this pair of houses the opposite is not just true, but reconciled in a profound meditation on the condition of living on a mountainside.

Right: **Two Houses, Ponte de Lima, Portugal.** Souto de Moura proves the dictum of his teacher, Fernando Tavora: "in architecture the opposite is also true"

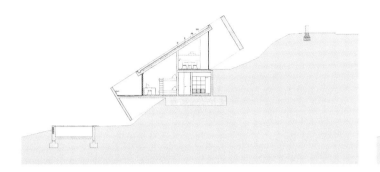
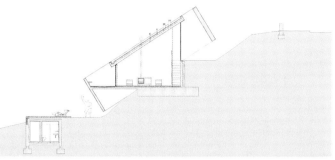

Casa Cascara

Cazú Zegers and Juan Pablo Almarza
Kawelluco, Chile 2002

With the Pacific Ocean on one side of their long, thin country and the Andes a very high and never too distant barrier on the other, Chileans like to repeat the saying that where Europeans have architecture, their monuments come from the terrain. Rarely less than dramatic and often outright spectacular, its elemental natural phenomena are inescapable and though Chile does, of course, have architecture and some very fine architects, it is underpinned by an engagement with nature. Looking towards an especially dramatic range of mountains Casa Cascara, in Kawelluco near the fashionable resort of Pucón some 800 kilometres south of the capital Santiago, takes this aspect of Chilean architecture to the extreme.

Though the town originated as a military base and became a trading centre as the European settlers gradually worked their way to the bottom of the enticingly beautiful country, by the middle of the twentieth century it had become a resort. It is not hard to see why. Here the Andes cluster around the active volcano of Villarica, the upper third of its 5000-foot height covered in glaciers while sulphurous smoke emanates from its crater. The lower slopes are covered with ancient forests while crystal-clear lakes form in their valleys.

Above: **Casa Cascara, Kawelluco, Chile.** The convex form of the entrance facade is naturally defensive, but a radial wall indicates the position of the front door and leads visitors towards it

Left: **Casa Cascara, Kawelluco, Chile.** A sketch by Cazú Zegers, showing the idea of a long low base to the vertical natural features, trees and mountains

Right: **Casa Cascara, Kawelluco, Chile.** This
sketch shows the concept of a shelter protected
by horizontal layers

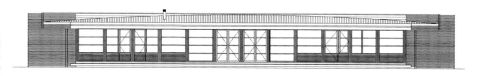

Right: **Casa Cascara, Kawelluco, Chile.**
Contrasting elevations, clearly showing the closed
and open nature of the two facades – enclosed
and protective to the south *(top)* and open on the
sun-facing north *(bottom)*

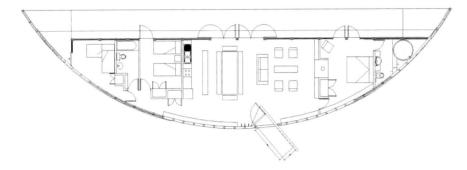

Left: Casa Cascara, Kawelluco, Chile. The plan is simple and logical, with living spaces in the centre, where the space is deepest, and bedrooms on both sides where the shape tapers toward either end

Right: **Casa Cascara, Kawelluco, Chile.** The main living space, viewed through the two-sided fireplace that also opens onto the main bedroom. Timber gives a warm and relaxing interior.

Above: **Casa Cascara, Kawelluco, Chile.** Another sketch, showing the intention of making the house almost invisible in the luscious forest.

Opposite: **Casa Cascara, Kawelluco, Chile.** The long, sheltered verandah emphasises the expansive view towards the mountains

Popular with affluent Chileans, pleasure seekers can raft, bike, hike, or go game fishing or snow boarding, all common contemporary reasons for living in, or at least having access to, the countryside.

Casa Cascara is one of several houses designed by Cazú Zegers and Juan Pablo Almarza in Kawelluco, a resort development set in a large private park about 15 minutes out of Pucón. All use a local wood called Coigüe which is similar to European beech and its colour is essentially light brown though the hue can vary from pale pink to yellow or red. Local builders understand this material and work comfortably with it which helps not just to keep costs down but also to intensify the connection between house and context. Cazú Zegers explains that the aim was to invest design and construction with a matching economy of approach. She achieves the first by making the house a single formal gesture and opening it to the view, while the latter comes through the use of a local and locally understood material, but with a refined simplicity well beyond the scope of most vernacular builders. The design challenges the potential of this wood to create a subtle volume, to screen and enclose space, and even to become something close to translucent.

Kawelluco consists of 1200 hectares of virgin wood. Two thirds of it are destined to become a park, while the remaining 400 hectares are slowly being developed with large, single family holiday homes, each set in its own clearing within the forest. Zegers' designs are variants on a theme – her long, mainly low-lying buildings present a solid face to the entrance and open towards the views. Despite their relatively simple construction technique, they use subtle and sophisticated geometry based on the arc of a circle intersected by straight lines to create a sense of illusion and mystery.

The timber is detailed and shaped to fit the formal concept: for example, it is laid horizontally to emphasise the long, low form, while the horizontal strips project slightly beyond the vertical post, as if to melt away into the surrounding forest. This is also far from vernacular, but is instead a very graphic illustration of the idea that scenery, rather than architecture, is what

creates monuments in Chile. Set on the edge of a wooded area, where the houses are situated, its form and detail focus the house inexorably towards the group of mountains in the middle distance. Towards its approach it presents a convex curve, and though as night falls its interior glows enigmatically through the openings in the facade, its linear form makes it not much more than a socle against the undulating peaks beyond. The horizontally laid timber strips serve to heighten the contrast with the upward thrust of the mountains, whose presence permeates the design. At its ends the timber narrows to suggest a fading into that natural setting. Where a vernacular building would merge organically with its surroundings, this house has been consciously designed to create a moment of awe, when all sensibilities are suspended in the presence of nature.

Viewed from the main entrance the house seems to be closed and resistant to penetration, apart from a short wall which projects outwards on a radial line. This leads to the recessed front door. Once beyond the walls, the house assumes a completely different character. What from the outside was a convex curve, visually pushing the visitor away, becomes a concave form serving to focus and gather attention on the mountains. As if in confirmation,

Above: **Casa Cascara, Kawelluco, Chile.**
Where the entrance facade jealously guards the house's privacy, the private elevation facing north towards the sun is expansive before its edges fade into the background

the north facade facing the sun – for this is the southern hemisphere – is a largely glazed straight line, with a covered external boardwalk that incorporates space for hammocks. The interior has a warmth that can only come from wood. Its plan is the residual space of a circle with a chord drawn across it; lying along the straight line of the chord, the north elevation provides a strong armature from which to organise what are, in any case, fairly simple interior spaces. Making this facade largely transparent and openable allows both views and internal movement to follow the promise of the southern concave wall and focuses attention towards the mountains. Taking advantage of the maximum bulge of the curve the living room is located at the centre, with a kitchen area to one side and bedrooms at either end.

There are all sorts of environmental and economic reasons for using local materials and local labour when building a holiday resort in such a fabulous natural landscape. But Casa Cascara and its companions show that that need not mean excising innovative architectural ideas. On the contrary, by introducing curves and intensifying established construction techniques, Zegers' designs reinforce the starting point of Chilean architecture, that its monuments lie in the landscape to which architecture is subservient.

Well Hall

Qingyun Ma
Jade Valley, Xian, China   2002

In Chinese culture nature is intimately connected to the cosmos, so altering or inserting anything into it becomes an act laden with significance. Though China's rapidly changing social and economic infrastructure may appear to be sweeping away all traces of her history and age-old belief systems, Qingyun Ma's Well Hall, lying some 35 kilometres south of the ancient capital of Xian, shows how the country's traditional dwellings can adapt and evolve into that quintessentially modern phenomenon, the vacation house for city dwellers. If the ever increasing numbers of China's 1.3 billion population who are now moving into her exponentially expanding cities represent the greatest challenge yet to conventional ideas of urbanism, this project offers an opportunity to reflect on the inverse of that phenomenon.

Few architects are as engaged with China's ongoing urbanisation as Ma. A string of projects from his Shanghai-based practice, MADA, shows the influence of his erstwhile collaborator Rem Koolhaas in the way they address the effects of rapid development, and indeed this may be the only strategy appropriate to such conditions. In the countryside it is different. The setting of Well Hall resonates with significance for Chinese history and tradition. It is situated in Jade Valley, whose boundaries are the Qinling mountain range and the Guanzhong plain, two contrasting and imposing topographical features that together create a highly varied landscape, from steep mountains to gentle slopes and the valley of the River Wei He. Green fields of wheat stretch to the horizon in every direction.

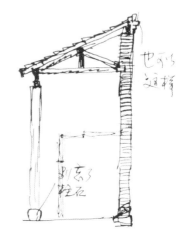

Above: **Well Hall, Jade Valley, Xian, China.**
As the house was built with local labour, which follows traditional construction practices, Ma used freehand sketches to explain what he wanted to the builders

Left: **Well Hall, Jade Valley, Xian, China.**
Another of Ma's sketches: this one shows an elevation of the rooms facing the entrance courtyard

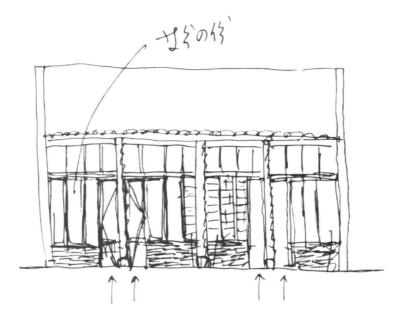

Opposite: **Well Hall, Jade Valley, Xian, China.**
In keeping with Chinese tradition, the house presents an austere face to the outside, with only a vestigial porch over the entrance

Left: **Well Hall, Jade Valley, Xian, China.**
Well Hall has a commanding site, but seems
to blend into the landscape

Nor should the area be considered merely a catalogue of landscape
features, for it is also a cradle of humanity and civilisation. Here lived the
prehistoric 'Lantian man'; it was the local jade deposits that supplied the
material for one of China's most important cultural traditions, while Xian was
the eastern end of the Silk Road, the ancient trading route which brought the
wonders of Chinese civilisation westwards and ultimately to a still barbarous
Europe. Like Rome, Xian is known as the 'eternal city'; its 4000 ancient ruins
testify to its 3100-year history and the 13 dynasties which made it their
capital. Even the footfall of more than a billion people moving east and south
to the coastal plains and their vast cities cannot erode either the area's natural
beauty or the human history that is so deeply inscribed into a land that
nurtured so many longstanding beliefs and traditions.

Just as an ebbing tide drags the sand back to reveal the true form of
otherwise hidden rocks, so the tide of humanity flowing into China's cities
offered Ma an opportunity to consider what the essence of a Chinese country
house might be. Only then could it be updated for today, and this is implied
in the house's name. He explains that 'Well' is often used to denote a
courtyard space which is open to the sky, while 'Hall' is the traditional term
for the social part of a private house; it also reflects the concept of a family

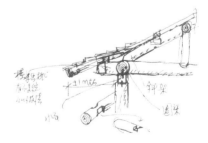

Above: **Well Hall, Jade Valley, Xian, China.**
Sketch showing roof construction

Right: **Well Hall, Jade Valley, Xian, China.** A single composition fom the outside, a central cross-wall inside separates the house from a courtyard garden

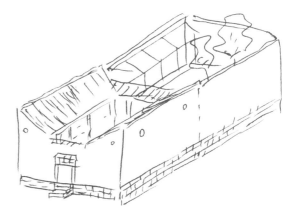

Below: **Well Hall, Jade Valley, Xian, China.** The forbidding exterior conceals rooms and courtyards inside, an allegorical representation of paradise

unit as an analogue of the cosmos. The clients were family friends and being part of their social circle gave Ma an insight into how traditional notions of the Chinese home might be adapted for their particular needs.

The site is commanding in a way that would have resonated equally as much with the Ancient Greeks as it does with contemporary Chinese. They knew that it is not necessary to be on the highest point to control a space; what matters is visibility, and Well Hall has a 360-degree prospect to distant mountains whose appearance changes with each of the four seasons. Outwardly the house presents an almost impenetrable grey brick wall with minimal openings. It has a deliberately rough and elemental character, reinforcing its role as a protective shell, and so it supports the traditional Chinese idea of the interior as a representation of paradise. But this is paradise in a secular and modern age, where interaction between people is more satisfying than communing with deities. Accordingly the social part of the house is an adaptation rather than a copy of traditional Chinese architectural norms. As Ma writes, "we have remodelled the residential quarter and social quarter, altered the interior spatial formation, changed brick courses and readjusted the fenestration schemes", to suit the dynamic of a modern family rather than to appease ancient deities.

The front door leads into a long, narrow courtyard, its floor pebbled and its sides defined by timber screens marking off suites of rooms on either side.

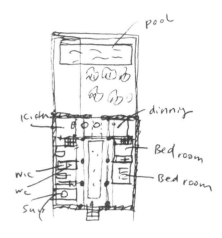

Above: **Well Hall, Jade Valley, Xian, China.** An early design sketch, showing the general layout of the house and the 'hidden' courtyard garden

Left: **Well Hall, Jade Valley, Xian, China.** The principal space within the walls is the large, bare courtyard, a place for contemplation where the sun's shadow creates a connection to nature and the cosmos

Right: **Well Hall, Jade Valley, Xian, China.** View from the entrance, which leads to a narrow court flanked by ranges of accommodation, and itself leads into the main courtyard visible through the far doorway

Below: **Well Hall, Jade Valley, Xian, China.**
Well Hall is only the latest human habitation in a
spectacular landscape where humans and their
immediate ancestors have lived for a million years

Right: **Well Hall, Jade Valley, Xian, China.**
Diagrammatic site plan, showing the contours, a
nearby settlement, rice fields and the river

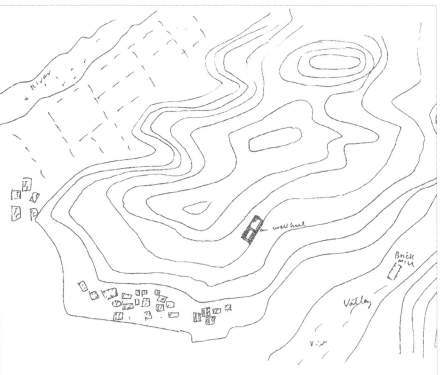

Its shape makes it strongly axial and invites movement towards another door at the far end. This leads into a range of rooms that run across the width of the house and form the main social spaces, including the kitchen and dining room. Beyond the dining room lies another courtyard, this time occupying the full width of the perimeter rectangle and reaching to its far end. Accounting for nearly half the area within the outer wall, it is protected from the outside though placed at the north-eastern corner to take advantage of the sun entering from the south and the prospect towards the mountains to the north. What from the outside seemed a simple rectangle is transformed on the inside into a more complex sequence of spaces, each taking its character from its shape and prospect.

Such complexities continue into a more intimate scale. The rooms which flank the narrow courtyard, services to one side and bedrooms to the other, have monopitched roofs which slope upwards to the edge, creating space for an open sleeping loft and reading gallery. Also at this level are two glass pavilions affording 360-degree panoramic views. Invisible from the outside, they are open but private, in contrast to the ground floor which is enclosed but configured for communal interaction. A nuclear family, not ancestral tradition, has become the standard measure and the basis of a new cosmology. The occupants of this house may not believe in the literal truth of the ancient beliefs that natural phenomena were the dwelling places of celestial beings, though since their needs have been placed at the centre of the design process, they may feel a little like that themselves.

House in the Tian Shan Mountains

Audrey Matlock

Almaty, Kazakhstan 2006

Designing a country house in the foothills of the Tian Shan Mountains, the range that forms the dividing line between Kazakhstan and China, provides plenty of scope for Audrey Matlock to demonstrate her belief that architecture should be about investigation. Vast and sparsely populated, Kazakhstan has little indigenous tradition of country house building. Most of its inhabitants were pastoral nomads until the Russians arrived, bringing with them the idea of permanent architecture: initially orthodox cathedrals and other paraphernalia of Tsarism; latterly the sort of concrete residential slabs that can be found anywhere from Vilnius to Vladivostok. In tune with the times, the country's largest city Almaty – which lies some way below the house, in the mountainous east of a country that is largely flat Steppe – has started to spawn suburban sprawl. However, quite what constitutes the Kazakh country house of today – or indeed of yesterday and tomorrow – is an open question.

Matlock's investigations had to include two specific issues. Having grown up in the Soviet era the clients, a real estate developer and his wife, knew what they did not want, while the international nature of his business had introduced him to a variety of possibilities in terms of quality and finish. Matlock had to find a way of harnessing that determined desire for innovation in cultural terms, in particular the introduction of a sense of space and light, to the dramatic and relatively remote site. The second issue came from the nature of the site itself, for while the mountain scenery is unquestionably

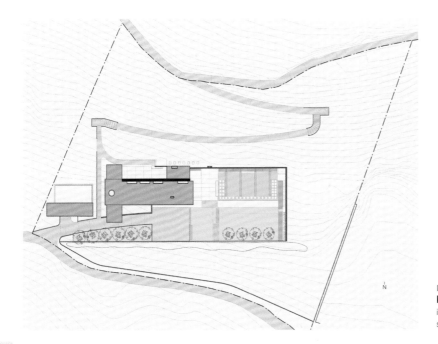

Right: House in the Tian Shan Mountains, Kazakhstan. The house seems to carve a precinct for itself in the mountainside, an oasis of order in rugged nature

Left: House in the Tian Shan Mountains, Kazakhstan. Site plan: the mountainside setting is spectacular but unstable, with a complicated set of retaining walls to stabilise it

spectacular, the ground is unfortunately highly unstable. Several times in the twentieth century Almaty was almost destroyed by earthquakes and other seismic-related catastrophes such as mud slides and floods when natural dams in the high mountain valleys burst. Hence, putting a home of any description on the steeply inclined site required the construction of extensive retaining walls almost encircling the entire site. The resulting terraces suggest a taming of the rugged landscape into a formal precinct in which the house sits, and the massively solid earthworks bring something of the angular precision of the house to the immediate outdoor spaces, blurring the distinction between inside and out, between nature and artifice.

Below: **House in the Tian Shan Mountains, Kazakhstan.** A cross section *(below)* and a long section *(centre)* through the house, with the main elevation *(bottom)*. Cut into the hillside, the house has three main levels: a swimming pool whose front wall opens onto a walled courtyard; a main level with reception rooms and terrace garden; and a bedroom floor above

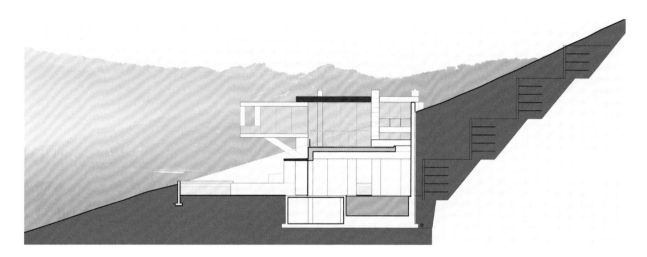

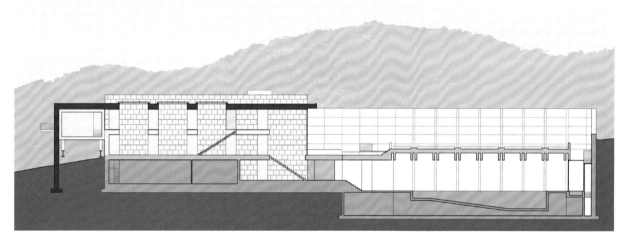

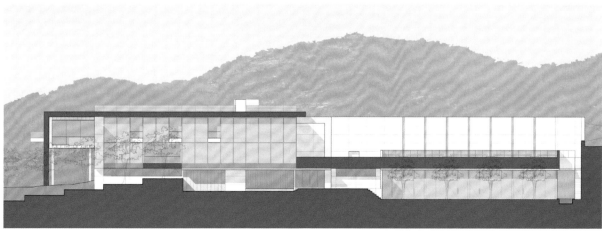

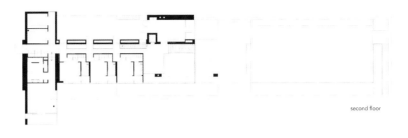

second floor

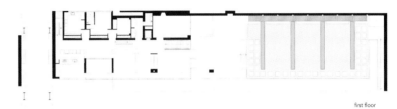

first floor

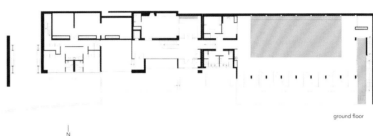
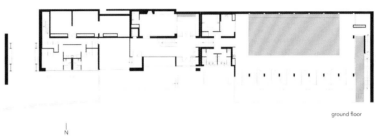

ground floor

N

Retaining walls announce the house from the approach while a driveway takes visitors past a guardhouse to the entrance situated at the centre of the precinct. At this, the lowest level, few of the house's spatial qualities are apparent: the swimming pool on the same floor remains concealed behind a hedge, while the rest of the floor contains ancillary accommodation such as staff rooms, plant and the garage. A small courtyard lies on axis with the entrance while at right angles a straight flight of steps leads to the main level. This acts as a platform, static within the implied and potential dynamism of the mountainside, with formally disposed internal and external spaces arranged running east–west and so more or less following the contour of the south-facing site. The living, sitting and dining rooms face south, though the first also has an eastern view over the grassed terrace towards distant snow-capped mountains. Behind them is a circulation spine and on its other side, cut into the hillside, are more private spaces, including a den and guest bedroom. On the top floor are a playroom and three bedrooms for children, as well as the main suite with its bedroom cantilevered over the entrance court and its bathroom and dressing areas reaching back into the mountainside. Each bedroom has its own mountain-view terrace: the main suite's at the end of the cantilever, and for the children's rooms the terraces are tucked into an angle between bedroom and bathroom.

With its long and relatively low shape and intimate connection with its site and the wider landscape, the house has a touch of Frank Lloyd Wright, whose work is also called to mind by the internal planning. Although most spaces are essentially rectilinear, the pure forms are only implied. Their corners erode into windows or other spaces, allowing a continual and intriguing flow between them. As much as dividing rooms, walls indicate and frame views, a principle that is continued in the formal garden outside the main living room and above the swimming pool. Here walls and hedges provide shelter and protection but also point towards distant peaks.

Turning programmatic requirements and site conditions into determinants of the design is a venerable Modernist strategy, and Matlock sees her particular interpretation of Modernism as a way of investigating what a contemporary Kazakh country house could be. The absence of any living tradition undermines the authenticity of any precedent; instead, the way the occupants' aspirations and the dynamic between them interact with the site and the stimuli it offers are the surest starting point.

Matlock characterises the main programmatic aims as "comfort, function and a healthy lifestyle". Spatial variety provides the basis for comfort, as different spaces cater for changing moods, while the flow between them suggests that these states of mind do not exist in total isolation. In turn, this interflow has implications for the relationships between occupiers – and certainly allows more possibilities to evolve than a small, poorly constructed apartment. The house offers scope for the family to develop its own balance. As there are also resident servants and guards, those relationships extend beyond an immediate nuclear family, hinting at the emergence of a more complex but organic society. Underlining this point is the possibility of building a recreation building, perhaps a proto-country club, for friends and neighbours. Finally a healthy lifestyle might start with the easy flow between inside and outside spaces, but it reaches its apogee in the 20-metre-long swimming pool which, though fully enclosed for year-round use, has one long wall which opens completely onto an enclosed garden.

In short, one definition of the house is as the realisation of an investigation into what happens when the internal dynamic of a microcosm of contemporary Kazakh society is placed against a backdrop of Kazakh landscape. At an immediate level the interaction can hardly fail to be successful, as the house provides for an enviable, relaxed and healthy lifestyle in stunning surroundings. But it also has the potential to go further: to show more broadly how an architecture that eschews tainted or irrelevant references can become a constituent part of a new society.

Right: **House in the Tian Shan Mountains, Kazakhstan.** Interior view of the double-height living room, overlloking the terrace garden to one side and the mountains on the other

Above: **House in the Tian Shan Mountains, Kazakhstan.** An alternative view of the living room *(top)*, overlooked by a glass wall to the bedroom floor above, and the terrace garden at night *(above)* offering opportunities for alfresco dining

Left: **House in the Tian Shan Mountains, Kazakhstan.** View from the entrance: the house is approached up a hill, past the guardhouse and under the cantilevered main bedroom

FOREST

House outside Moscow

Tanya Kalinina of McAdam Architects

near Moscow, Russia   2000

With the collapse of the Soviet Union and its former territories' discovery of the fruits of capitalism, one unforeseen effect of the dramatic upheaval has been the emergence of a new kind of country house. Tanya Kalinina and her English partner James McAdam estimate that the proportion of Moscow residents who can afford to spend lavishly on their homes might now be as high as 10 per cent, though few own a football club on the side. As this affluent social group did not exist under communism, their architectural tastes have quite different characteristics to those of previous owners of Russian country houses. The magazine *Project Russia* hinted at the motivations for building such homes in an issue devoted to new country houses in 2001, suggesting that such dwellings offered something between the urban polarities of Bohemian unconventionality and bourgeois comforts. Kalinina adds that pollution in Moscow is another reason to escape, but these factors alone do not create a new building type. This house outside Moscow, finished at the turn of the millennium, shows one direction the type could take.

Architecture is almost always a cause of dilemma for new elites. Being new merely emphasises their arriviste credentials, and while borrowing from history might strengthen their claims to status it does little to reflect their personal achievements. When that history is as tainted as that of the Soviet Union, as a frame of reference it is even less appealing. Although retreating to one's dacha was a relatively common way of alleviating the drab uniformity

Above: **House outside Moscow, Russia.** The house has a wooded 18-hectare site outside Moscow

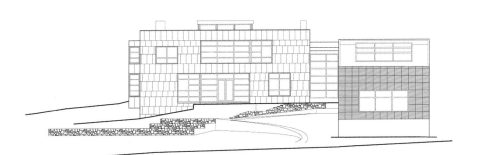

Left: **House outside Moscow, Russia.**
Elevations: the north-west-facing entrance front *(top)*, and the south-east-facing front *(bottom)*. Much of the stone was imported, showing the lengths Russia's new clients will go to to obtain the effects they want

Above: **House outside Moscow, Russia.** The large, L-shaped house set amid pine trees recalls Alvar Aalto's Villa Mairea

and privations of daily existence that were strongly manifested in architecture – "the contrast of the Soviet concrete box and the self-made dacha couldn't be stronger," reported *Project Russia* – these little huts hardly reflected their owners' understandable aspirations for luxury. Delving further back into history presented another kind of difficulty. By the turn of the millennium the country estates familiar to Chekov, Turgenev and Tolstoy had passed out of living memory, and the long hiatus in private commissions means that the attempts to recreate such dwellings from the past tend to be crass.

Social change often brings a change in patterns of taste, albeit with a necessarily direct correlation between them. When a society with ambitions to control all aspects of its citizens' lives implodes, that sense of unpredictability increases. In Russia there is no orthodoxy in terms of architecture and potential clients look to all manner of influences. Within them, perhaps most obviously in the *Wallpaper*-reading subgroup, Kalinina and McAdam have found several clients for large, contemporary country houses. Travelled but not necessarily cultured (*kultiviert*) and always clever and energetic, they can pick up ideas and interests rapidly from numerous

Right: **House outside Moscow, Russia.** The double-height reception hall runs the full width of the house

Above: **House outside Moscow, Russia.** Ground-floor and part site plan. The simple layout uses size to create effects: the fully serviced kitchen is to the left of the entrance

Opposite: **House outside Moscow, Russia.** Given Moscow's extreme climate, the reception hall doubles as a winter garden. The detailing was kept simple throughout the house to accommodate the available skills of the local construction industry

disparate influences, whether magazines, a visit to Switzerland or the French Riviera. The country, they say, is like America a century ago, rich but with few examples among its building stock.

In essence, the demands of clients for their new country houses also have parallels with those of twelfth-century castle builders, the 'new men' who commissioned the Elizabethan 'prodigy houses', or Nicolas Fouquet who built Vaux-le-Vicomte – it is incumbent on them to make a statement about their occupants' position within the evolving social heirarchy. In this context new country houses have not only to reflect an individual's status, but also to draw imaginatively on the possibilities of nature. It goes without saying that neither frame of reference was a priority for the old state-run design institutes.

Many of their requirements start with considerations of practical and functional manifestations, such as size, with 1000 square metres being quite common, or the need to incorporate a large indoor swimming pool together with the obligatory Jacuzzi. Another characteristic is the need to accommodate servants, with dedicated living quarters on site, calling for a skill in organisational planning of the type that won William Burn many a commission from nineteenth-century British oligarchs, but was a talent that had little cachet in the former Soviet Union. Finally, security as well as the supply of water and energy are often important issues. To these factors must be added the nature of the Russian countryside itself; around Moscow it is largely flat, often forested, with rivers as the only major natural features, and is subject to extreme variations in climate.

Set in a thickly wooded 18-hectare site which undulates between rocky mounds, Kalinina's house is made up of two forms which are, on plan, essentially simple rectangles: one long and thin for the swimming pool, the other almost square and containing the main accommodation. Two devices modify the formal purity. One is a direct reflection of the topography, allowing the swimming pool volume to follow the slope. The other is contrived as a way of mediating between the interior and exterior: windows are important here. Some, such as those at low level in the pool room, give an indication of the function within, in this case because they are placed at the swimmers' eye level. In framing views they also forge a connection between the internal spaces and external features on the site.

Allowing the house and its inhabitants to exist within rather than above nature was a central concern of the design and has also influenced the main block. It has a central, double-height winter garden with the main living accommodation on either side, the kitchen and dining room to one side and further reception rooms on the other. That this basic *parti* has much in common with generic Palladian villa plans is probably no coincidence. Palladio's influence runs so strongly through the Western tradition of country houses that scarcely an architect can be unaware of it, even if they choose to reject it. This enduring influence stems in part from the practicality of Palladio's plans, both functionally and as a means of expressing the position of a class that, if not new to power, had only recently taken to the pleasures of rural life.

Also like Palladio's villas, this house had to adapt to the capabilities of the local construction industry. Detailing and features such as the internal staircase had to be kept simple, but that imposed a certain practical elegance on them. Here the strategy for covering up the inevitable roughness of local masonry was to import a smooth limestone cladding. This gives the house a precision and prominence within its forest setting, establishing a visual tension between nature and artifice that might prove a starting point for a revived tradition of Russian country houses.

Above: **House outside Moscow, Russia.**
A generous swimming pool and Jacuzzi, more commonly found in luxury hotels in the west, are *de rigueur* for Russian oligarchs

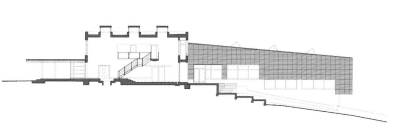

Left: **House outside Moscow, Russia.**
Sections, through the pool *(left)* and through the reception hall *(below),* with the swimming pool wing in elevation

Opposite: **House outside Moscow, Russia.**
The sloping ceiling and rooflights create a playful pattern of light which becomes animated as swimmers disturb the water surface

Duckett House

John Pardey
New Forest, Hampshire   2003

John Pardey belongs to a small group of English architects who are trying to establish a contemporary idiom for rural homes whose scale puts them somewhere between the traditional elitist country house and the mass market dwelling. These homes are perhaps the closest equivalent today to the type of houses in which Jane Austen's characters would have lived. They have similar generic accommodation, with two or three reception rooms and bedrooms that would certainly become overcrowded if more servants than a nanny had to be fitted in alongside a clutch of children. And, like many of Austen's characters, their occupants choose to live in the country even though their income does not derive directly from the land. The difference, of course, is in the architecture: where her lesser clergymen, half-pay officers

and presumptuous merchants chose to mimic the building style of their grander, landowning neighbours and thereby gain acceptance, Pardey's designs seek to develop an affinity with nature by relating form and materials to their surroundings. In this sense the context they address is physical, whereas Austen's characters and contemporaries were intent on conforming to its social counterpart. This change in approach liberates and enriches the potential for architectural expression, and Pardey's eclectic reading of Modernism and rarefied feel for the vernacular allow him to exploit it.

The Duckett House, on the edge of the New Forest close to the southern coast of England, is in many senses typical of this genre of new country houses. Its clients are a professional couple with young children; when they made the not uncommon move from London to the country, they were fortunate enough to find a site with potential to become a rural idyll, while still being close enough to employment opportunities afforded by the prosperous cities on the south coast. The site is attractive rather than spectacular, and there appears little artifice in the surrounding landscape beyond what is necessary for farming. Local agricultural buildings, too recent to be genuinely vernacular, provide the cue for the volumes and, to some extent, the textures of the design, but the house is conceived in a way which is clearly contemporary; its large windows show how that sense of the new continues to the relaxed and comfortable interior. At one edge of the site, though, are some rather run-down agricultural structures and they give a clue to the way the project ran the gauntlet of the British planning system, which often considers any trace of modernity to be threatening even when it has a pitched roof and plenty of timber cladding.

The site was a smallholding and planning consent is more likely to be forthcoming for replacing a building – in this case a decrepit agricultural

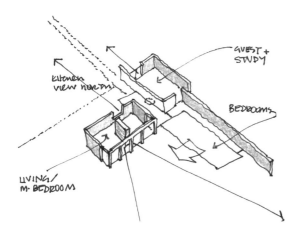

GUEST + STUDY

Kitchen view north

BEDROOMS

LIVING/ M. BEDROOM

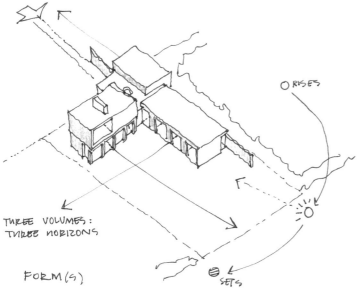

○ RISES

THREE VOLUMES: THREE HORIZONS

FORM(S)

○ SETS

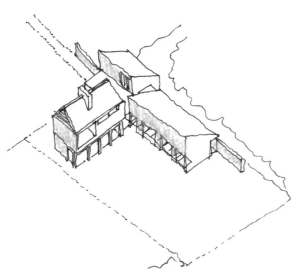

Above: **Duckett House, New Forest, Hampshire, UK.** Seen from the private garden the house becomes almost transparent

cottage – than for starting on an entirely new site. By the same token there is an incentive to keep even the most tumbledown buildings because at some point, something new might be considered an acceptable trade-off for removing an eyesore. Fortunately, the site is large enough for these structures not to impinge on the house's immediate environment, though they provide useful extra storage and make a convenient point to limit car access. The clients' willingness not to take cars right to the house meant that Pardey could design its approach as a long footpath, and that became an important generator of the concept.

The path makes a straight armature swathing through grass which is not treated as a lawn. Just before reaching the house it acquires a low wall on one side, emphasising the direction and protecting a study from unwanted visitors. From this point onwards the armature helps to define the three basic volumes of the house, each related to a specific function, which interlock in the overall composition. One is the study and a guest bedroom, which together could make a nearly self-contained suite. Another, to the right of the entrance, is the principal volume: two storeys with a sitting room and double-height kitchen/dining area on the ground floor, and the main bedroom above. The third, continuing the axis of the entrance, is a run of four children's bedrooms.

It is a skilful and attractive composition. From the approach it is welcoming and legible, the entrance clearly visible while the massing and windows give clues to the purposes of the various parts. Inside it offers both privacy and intimacy. The entrance sequence of path, porch and hall means that visitors only penetrate in stages, and some parts, like the study or bedrooms, can remain totally private. Yet in the L-shaped angle formed by the children's wing and the main block, the house opens up to a lawn, which is banked up to be more or less flat. The wall from the sitting room and kitchen is entirely glazed and opens up to the lawn; the children's bedrooms each have a stable door to afford graded privacy from the rest of the family. At first glance the site appears to be mainly natural, but in fact it has been subtly manipulated to reinforce these spatial characteristics.

Other touches in the plan show a sensitivity to how the house might be used. The position of the children's bathroom at the end of their wing suggests a relationship with the garden that might just, for the very young, provide a substitute for a swimming pool. Along the corridor, too, a small widened section – some double the width – makes the sort of place that children can take over for their games, with just the kind of secret views they so enjoy.

In the Duckett House and others that explore similar themes of composition, Pardey begins to set out a new typology for medium-sized rural housing. Its forms are derived from the vernacular, and its materials combine large areas of glass with more traditional render and timber, a device that helps to ease a path through draconian and conservative planning regulations. More significantly, it also opens the door to imaginative layouts and configurations of space that cater well for family life in the twenty-first century, and help to bring that social organism into some sort of relationship with the environment where they have chosen to live. As many of these families will have faced the choice of a five-metre-wide terraced house in a London suburb, the contrast is great – and will become greater if Pardey's typological essays are not compromised by conservative planners.

Below: **Duckett House, New Forest, Hampshire, UK.** Section through the double-height kitchen/dining area, with the children's bedroom wing in elevation

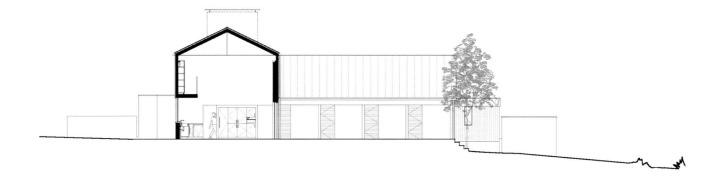

Forest Floor House

Kengo Kuma
Nagano, Japan   2004

The floor in Kengo Kuma's Forest Floor House, a vacation house near Nagano, is not the forest floor itself but a platform floating 2.6 metres above it. Elevated on this artificial platform the house's inhabitants live among the foliage which seems to provide the outer limits of its spaces, as if surrounded by billowing clouds or waves of green. Yet this is far from primeval tree-dwelling. The floor itself begins to take on the role of organising and defining space, even of mediating between different cultural traditions, and so the design turns the experience of living in a natural setting into a reflection on life in the twenty-first century.

Updating Japanese tradition to suit contemporary living is a particular theme of Kuma's work. His Louis Vuitton Moët Hennessy headquarters in Tokyo is the first building in the city in decades to use wood as its main external material, a choice made possible by a powerful sprinkler system; though its detailing and appearance are contemporary, at a deeper level it recalls the tradition of timber construction. But it is the role of the floor that fascinates Kuma most. In traditional Japanese architecture the floor and roof had greater symbolic and functional value than the walls, and the floor in particular, with devices like *tatami* mats, set out and regulated how the

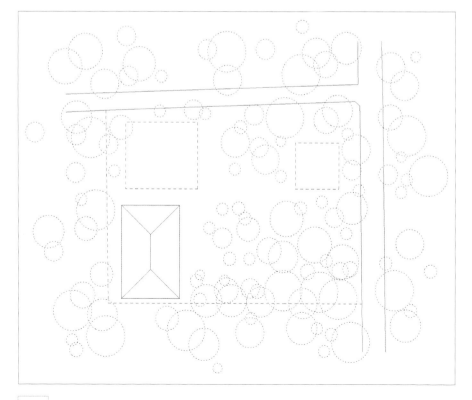

Left: **Forest Floor House, Nagano, Japan.**
Site plan: the house is set well back from the road, its transparency protected by dense woodland

spaces could be used. In the late nineteenth and early twentieth centuries, there was an entire strand of Japanese architecture called *sukiya-zukuri* which was devoted to the art of the floor deriving from the highly ritualised custom of drinking tea.

Outside the sphere of domestic design, the floor is even more important. Spurred by several commissions to design Noh theatres, Kuma has made a particular study of this traditional Japanese dramatic form, and his designs concentrate on presenting the floor as a symbol of and platform for performing its near ritualistic roles. The backdrop is not, as it would be in Western theatre, artificial scenery, but the trees of the forest, while the emotional state of the actors is determined by their positions on the stage. These ideas began to come together in domestic design with his spectacular Glass/Water House on the Atami coast (1995), seemingly a platform floating on concentric rings of water which move from still to turbulent the further they are from the centre.

Like the Glass/Water House, the Forest Floor House also weaves in a layer of Western and specifically Modernist interests. As Kuma confesses, having chosen to create a house that floats in the forest, "the first thing that came to my mind was the Farnsworth House by Mies van der Rohe". Mies's design, though, Kuma continues, expresses itself through its steel frame which describes a box-like volume. A frame controls how the house allows its inhabitants to construct a relationship with nature.

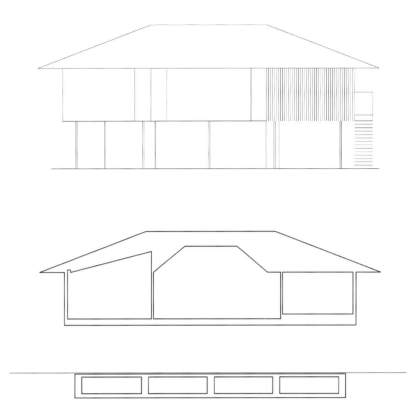

Right: **Forest Floor House, Nagano, Japan.**
Elevation *(top)*, showing the tea room adjacent to
the stairs, and section *(right)*: the roof hangs and
its eaves taper to a fine edge

Opposite: **Forest Floor House, Nagano,
Japan.** Dark and contemplative, the tea
room is an ideal environment to consider
the transience of nature

In contrast, Kuma explains, at Forest Floor House "I designed a floor, not a box". The vertical supports are minimal and easily lost when the house is seen through the trees. As the umbrella-like roof hangs from above, no columns interrupt the flow between inside and out, and the deeply overhanging eaves lose the glass walls in shadow. What exists is a horizontal layer contained between two flat planes, and a convenient undercroft to which cars and storage can be banished to keep the main floor as clear as possible. The main floor offers varied experiences of nature for the house's inhabitants to interpret or digest as they will, perhaps as far as turning them to reasoned reflection. Sight is the most important, but sound, touch and smell also help to define the spaces when the glazed walls are open. Kuma sums up his aim: "Mies wanted to create a transparent box, but I attempted to create a transparent experience."

All of this implies a cultural difference, and that becomes explicit in the planning of the house itself. At 123 square metres it is quite small, but still manages to combine Eastern and Western concepts of space. A stairway on one of the short sides leads to a terrace, which in turn leads to a living room, the largest area in the house. Its seductive Minimalism intensifies the contrast with leaf-dappled light and the rustling of leaves entering from the outside, but with its Western-style furniture it does not quite reach the Japanese art of turning such an experience into an ethereal idea. That is left to the tea room, timber lined and considerably more private, which is tucked in between the stairway and terrace where it is less displayed and readily accessible than the other spaces, such as a bedroom and kitchen which are visible from the entrance. If the glass walls and lack of columns mean that nature in its raw state enters the bedroom and living room, here the refined fruits of the forest – sawn timber – set the terms for appreciating nature, which can be allowed or excluded by opening and closing the rice paper screens at one end.

Kuma comes in a line of architects who have developed a dynamic and fruitful relationship between Western and Japanese tradition, a process which started in the 1860s but took on a new and extremely productive form when Modernism emerged in the first part of the twentieth century. Kuma himself brings a new dimension to that process. A generation younger than the Metabolists and nearly two on from Kenzo Tange, he studied at Tokyo and Columbia Universities, where he specialised in Japanese tradition. On returning to Japan he found the country immersed in the economic boom of

Below: **Forest Floor House, Nagano, Japan.**
Construction section: the structure is steel on a concrete base

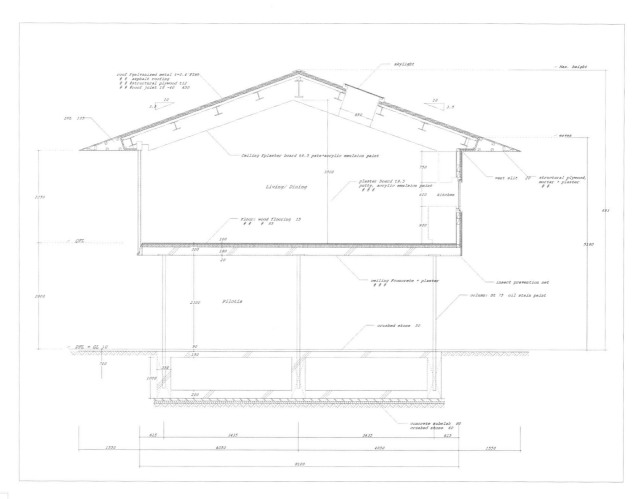

Above: Forest Floor House, Nagano, Japan.
Nature appears to have no impediment to flow into the house between floor and ceiling, not even a sofa arm

the 1980s. Only when that ended did he have the opportunity to contemplate the possibility of a more meaningful synthesis that had fascinated him at least since he became aware of the Japanese work of Bruno Taut. Taut's houses, dating from the 1930s, are a more subtle influence on Forest Floor House than the overt relationship with the Farnsworth House, and more pervasive throughout Kuma's oeuvre. But Taut never attempted something as daring as floating a house in the air, nor, dying in 1938, did he have the subsequent history of the twentieth century to address. In his knowing relationship with that history, Kuma indicates how a house can help to relate its inhabitants to nature in the twenty-first century.

Left: **Forest Floor House, Nagano, Japan.** In its immediate clearing the house has a powerful presence, shimmering as if transfigured by light

Below: **Forest Floor House, Nagano, Japan.** Plans of the ground-level undercroft *(bottom)* and the main floor *(top)*.

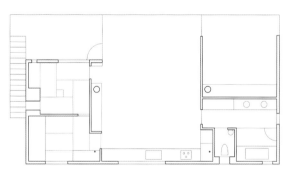

Mountain Tree House

Mack Scogin Merrill Elam Architects
Dilland, Georgia, USA   2001

As the family of the clients for Mack Scogin Merrill Elam's Mountain House, completed in 1996, grew up they acquired friends and grandchildren that contributed to a demand for more space in the ravishingly beautiful forested site in the southern Appalachian Mountains close to the state line between Georgia and North Carolina. So the clients, who have artistic interests, came back to the architects and asked for a second building, close by and related to the first, but introducing a subtly different aesthetic into those generic extension roles of guest accommodation and storage "for things like tractors and dogs", as the architects write.

Mountain House is quite large and, rising from a solid stone-clad base, it seems to stress its connection to the earth just as its flat roof emphasises its horizontality. Mountain Tree House repeats some of these motifs at smaller scale. It too has a solid base, this time in concrete, and a flat-roofed volume above, but it all seems to be stretched upwards, rather as the trees which surround it, straight and spindly, striving to grow fast and high in order to reach the sunlight they need to survive. And projecting to one side of the house, floating at first-floor level, is a Cor-Ten steel walled deck. Supported on slender columns that merge with the tree trunks, it lunges into the trees and seems to be buoyed up on the billows of their foliage. Though clearly related, the two buildings contrive their relationships between inside and out in quite different ways. In the main house it is geometry that dictates the spatial relationships, while the Mountain Tree House offers a more directly sensory experience of nature.

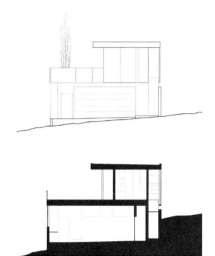

Above: **Mountain Tree House, Dilland, Georgia, USA.** Elevation *(top)* and cross-section *(above)*

Left: **Mountain Tree House, Dilland, Georgia, USA.** Site plan: the Mountain Tree House is to the top, the original Mountain House below

The basic accommodation is quite simple. A garage – "for the occasional car", but more often functioning as a workshop and store for garden tools – occupies the ground level. In keeping with its prosaic functions, its materials and forms are elemental: rough concrete shaped into a relatively simple volume. The principal space, a bedroom on the upper level, cantilevers over and commands the courtyard, but is reached via a concrete ramp which rises alongside the working area. Its materials emphasise its detachment; timber and steel framed with mainly glass walls, it is open and light compared to the earthbound garage on which it sits, with privacy coming from detachment rather than solid walls. Deep roof overhangs give it some shade, and its height makes it a vantage point from which to look back at the main house. A small bathroom opens off the bedroom. Though enclosed in the same steel as the deck and ramp hand-rails, its walls can swing open for open-air showers and other forms of communing with wind, trees and sunlight.

If a store and a spare bedroom are typical additions to an existing country house, a floating steel deck is not, and this is where the design leaves simple need behind and introduces new sensations. At nearly 100 square metres its area is more or less the same as the internal spaces, and is intended specifically as a place for sitting and looking, in contrast to the main house where spaces respond to needs which may be easier to define, like reading or displaying art. Here the observer is transported to a floating platform, but one where that most industrial of materials, self-weathering Cor-Ten steel, seems to mingle with the products of nature. Nor is it just a cage which separates nature from artifice, because through the black slate deck floor grow bamboo shoots, themselves rooted in a planter on the

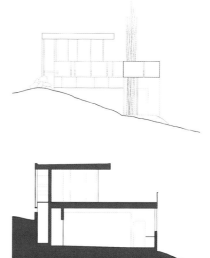

Above: **Mountain Tree House, Dilland, Georgia, USA.** Side elevation *(top)* and section *(below)*

ground. Quick growing, with their shapes and positions dictated by the design of the deck, their forms and colour reflect the trees beyond, and seem to suggest that on occasion and under some circumstances, nature can be subdued by architecture, just as the deck itself seems to disappear within the lush vegetation. The speed of their growth might even imply that this subjugation might be beneficial, as if the bamboo shoots are the design that will eventually be achieved in nature.

Mack Scogin Merrill Elam have a knack for creating satisfying complexity without becoming mannered. Scogin and Elam both worked for the large commercial architects and construction managers Heery & Heery – Scogin as president and in charge of design – before setting up their own firm in 1984. Their understanding of the strictures of commercial architecture taught them how to create effects without unduly increasing cost or difficulty of construction; having more than a foot in the more esoteric end of

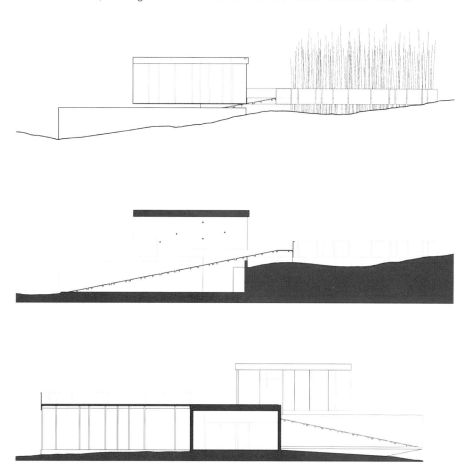

Right: **Mountain Tree House, Dilland, Georgia, USA.** Rear elevation *(top)*, section through the ramp between the glass screen and steel wall *(centre)*, and a section through the deck *(bottom)*

architecture as well, they had the insight to bring a real intellectual agenda to their design ability. Both have lectured and taught in schools of architecture across the US, and Scogin was chairman of the architecture department at Harvard's Graduate School of Design from 1990 to 1995. Armed with their experience at Heery & Heery, they realised how the client has a fundamental role in the quality of architecture, and, in their subsequent work, have shown how an ongoing dialogue with the client is not just a simple statement of need, but an essential strand in the weave that makes up imaginative design. The relationship that unfolded over several years with the client for Mountain House and Mountain Tree House is a good illustration.

Mountain Tree House shows how the relationship with site is another strand in the fabric. As the sense of lift shows, the design takes inspiration from the surrounding trees, though it does not purport to replicate or merge with nature. Instead, mediated through an understanding of the clients' desires, its relationship with the site is reflective and multi-tiered. In this way the design mingles personal traits with objective nature, and that, perhaps, goes some way to achieving Mack Scogin Merrill Elam's goal of an architecture whose meanings and interpretations are located within a broader cultural continuum than the narrow and self-referential concepts of truth to structure or materials.

Left: **Mountain Tree House, Dilland, Georgia, USA.** A ramp leads from the garage court to the deck and entrance to the bedroom

Above: **Mountain Tree House, Dilland, Georgia, USA.** Cantilevered over the garage court, the bedroom is enveloped in the tree canopy and has a view towards the main house

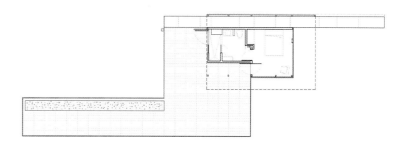

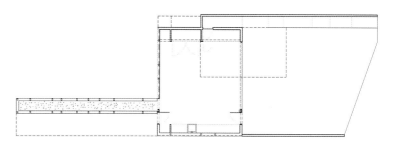

Right: **Mountain Tree House, Dilland, Georgia, USA.** Plans: garage level *(right)* and deck level *(above)*. Note the planter at low level for canes to grow through the deck above

OCEAN

House at Bay of Islands

Fearon Hay
Northland, New Zealand   1999

Ever since travel writing started in earnest in the eighteenth century, literature began to shape the way we look at nature; the development of photography in the nineteenth century and film in the twentieth accelerated the process to an extent that even the most remote parts of the world can now be rendered familiar and incorporated into a concept of landscape that is no less globalised and homogenised than urbanism. This is especially true of New Zealand, which has about 3.5 million inhabitants and a few million more visitors, though an exponentially greater number has become familiar with its spectacular scenery through films like the *Lord of the Rings* trilogy, even if they are largely unaware of where it is located.

Fearon Hay's house in the Bay of Islands, a north-easterly facing inlet in Northland – the finger that points north-west from the top of North Island – inverts this dynamic. As a work of architecture, it draws on an international language and brings this to bear on a specific location. Though even the finest designers in New Zealand would acknowledge that its own contribution to architectural culture is relatively small, they might also point out that the apparent simplicity of Modernism has some affinity and transformative potential for the more naive simplicity of the early settlers' shacks. So where film takes something from New Zealand and transforms it into part of a cultural language, Fearon Hay take another slice of international culture and adapt it to a particular manifestation of New Zealand's landscape. Its clean and crisp Modernist aesthetic becomes a counterpoint not just to the

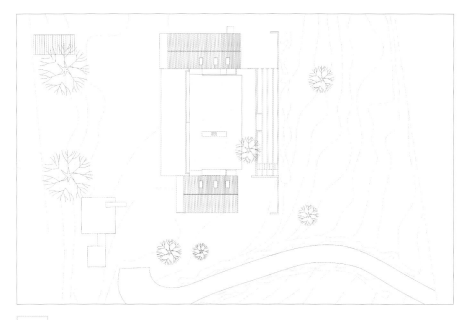

Left: House at Bay of Islands, Northland, New Zealand. Site plan: the site slopes down to the ocean

Opposite: House at Bay of Islands, Northland, New Zealand. The house enjoys a spectacular setting on a luscious and beautiful stretch of coast

Right: **House at Bay of Islands, Northland, New Zealand.** Cross section: the site slopes steeply behind the house forming a sheltered outdoor space, and more gently in front of it towards the ocean

wonderful setting, but to the whole way of looking at New Zealand's landscape in general. The history of this area adds more levels to the significance of these cultural travails. It was here that Europeans first settled the lush country and quickly came into contact with the Maoris who still make up almost a third of the local population. Here, too, the Treaty of Waitangi was signed, the first formal document to set out a relationship between the two cultures. No intervention in this location can avoid the interwoven strands of nature and culture, and on top of this the design must never ignore its primary purpose, of providing a comfortable and relaxing holiday home.

In that aim the house succeeds extraordinarily well. It was designed for a large family who frequently invite guests, who have plenty of room to stay in five first-floor bedrooms and a bunker room, modelled on a railway couchette on the ground floor. Situated a safe 28 metres from the mean level

Below: **House at Bay of Islands, Northland, New Zealand.** The glazed facades on both sides of the living room can be opened up completely to allow uninterrupted views of the magnificent prospect

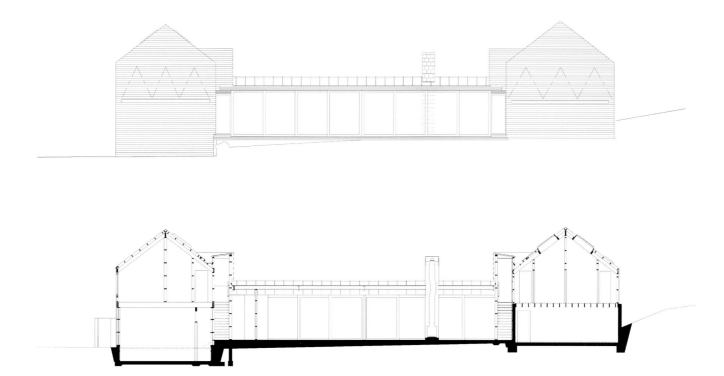

of spring tide high water, the land seems to flow down to the sea through the building, momentarily arrested by the minimally structured, single-storey living area. The elevation is just sufficient to give views beyond the immediate cove to the dramatic coastline on either side, and the lush greenery adds to the sense of relaxed comfort. While its aesthetic may be Modern, it still welcomes the inflow of nature. On the landward side above the house is a tennis court, a vantage point for overlooking the roof and grounds, and for gaining a sense of the wider landscape.

It would certainly be possible to enjoy the house just at this level, but it achieves these effects through deeper and more sophisticated consideration. Looking for a site where they would have plenty of space for boating and diving equipment, the clients bought this plot, which came with planning permission for a new house as well as an existing pair of two-storey, gabled boathouses about 20 metres apart. These offered ample storage but little in the way of aesthetic fulfilment, so they used them for a year while deciding what to do. When they went to Jeff Fearon and Tim Hay at the end of the 1990s, their young practice already had a commitment to Modernist aesthetics – though until then expressed only through urban projects. The two architects decided to keep the boathouses: they established the closest point a building could come to the sea while providing plenty of storage in naturally enclosed volumes. That point suited function and aesthetics; enclosure would also give privacy to the bedrooms on the first floor, and as solid forms they provided 'book-ends' at either end of a living area which could, consequently, be even more open than the Case Study Houses and the Barcelona Pavilion, which are clear if remote influences.

The form and construction of the two boathouses had something in common with the buildings occupied by the original European settlers, but recladding them with louvres and corrugated aluminium gives them a contemporary appearance. Each could almost be a small unit in itself, with two bedrooms above one and three on the other, though the ground floors are both largely stores, for boats and the bunk room on one side, a garage on the other. Between them is the 20-metre-long living space, separated into three zones: a kitchen, dining area and sitting room, with a large chimney dividing the last two. Almost nothing impedes their view eastwards to the sea and west onto the terraced slope of the land. As if to reinforce the flow between inside and out, the floor finish extends to a sheltered terrace at the rear and an open one overlooking the ocean. On both sides the glass walls slide back completely, so although this is a large house of almost 450 square metres on both floors, it appears to rest lightly on the ground, absorbing and refracting the boathouses into a greater conceptual harmony with the setting.

Yet, in this area where art and organic farming go hand in hand, the building is not so presumptuous as to pretend that it makes no impact. It recognises its status as a place for urbanites to relax and observe, and the consequent need to modify the natural environment. In using a Modernist design aesthetic to make a microcosm of New Zealand into something with very particular qualities for one family and their guests, the project shows how architecture might provide a dimension for looking at this wonderful piece of the world that film cannot.

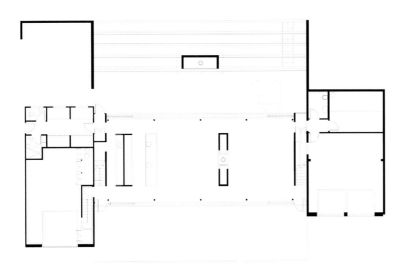

Left: **House at Bay of Islands, Northland, New Zealand.** Ground-floor plan. The boathouses enclose the service areas and storage for marine leisure equipment, leaving the living room to be as minimal as a Manhattan loft

Above: **House at Bay of Islands, Northland, New Zealand.** The large living room has a kitchen at one end, with a freestanding fireplace dividing the dining from the sitting areas

Left: **House at Bay of Islands, Northland, New Zealand.** First-floor plan, showing the main and guest bedrooms

Right: **House at Bay of Islands, Northland, New Zealand.** The design skilfully combines a minimal aesthetic with the practical advantages of large shed construction

McNair House

Sean Godsell

Mornington Peninsula, Victoria, Australia   2006

Few architects have approached their investigations into the concept of 'house' with the breadth and subtlety of the Australian architect Sean Godsell. Having spent time in Japan shortly after graduating in the mid-1980s, as well as with the die-hard British Modernist Denys Lasdun shortly afterwards, he is interested in synthesising elements of Eastern and Western domestic traditions, underpinned by a belief that a genuine Australian architecture can only emerge once the country recognises its geographic location as part of Asia. Another strand of his investigations concerns an interest in housing's visceral role as basic shelter, a purpose that affluence and professional aspirations can eclipse. He has explored these themes in Park Bench, a bench that opens into a night shelter for the urban homeless – which he entered for an award for the best new house in Australia – and Future Shack, a mobile shack that recycles shipping containers but shades them with a parasol to make a metal box habitable in inhospitable climes.

The McNair House shows how these interests can fruitfully combine. It comes in a line that includes projects such as the Carter Tucker House (1999) and Peninsula House (2002), both also in Victoria, whose Minimalism is more cultural than programmatic or budgetary than that of either shack or bench. But in striving to convey the essence of Eastern and Western traditions of domestic space, they suggest how the primal need for shelter might be met within those traditions – a subtle difference to the basic projects which imply that shelter might be so elemental as to exist outside any cultural tradition. Mapping this intellectual territory shows one side of Godsell's aim to help develop an authentically Australian architecture; another side, equally important and very apparent in the McNair House, is to combine climate and

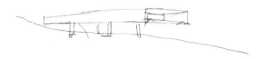

Above: McNair House, Mornington Peninsula, Victoria, Australia. Godsell's sketches show the idea of a long rectilinear volume resting on minimal supports

Left: McNair House, Mornington Peninsula, Victoria, Australia. Another sketch shows how the house can 'breathe', its sides opening like a fish's gills

Opposite: McNair House, Mornington Peninsula, Victoria, Australia. The house looms over its immediate surroundings to focus attention on the Southern Ocean

topography with primal needs and cultural expectations. It is literally a country house in the sense of being a rural home, but also in a deeper sense of looking towards a national architecture.

The house is located at St Andrew's Bay on the south coast of the Mornington Peninsula, which itself forms part of the southern edge of Port Phillip Bay, the inlet on Australia's south coast with Melbourne on its northern shore. Rarely for Australia, where much of the coast is owned by the state, at St Andrew's it is possible to build right on the foreshore, exposed to the full majesty of the ocean and its magnificent views and furious gales. The elevated site intensifies this condition and suggested a different sort of engagement with nature from those earlier houses that had nestled into the sand dunes. Instead, the McNair House is a long, thin oxidised steel-clad rectangle pointing straight out to sea and resting on a mere four columns. Here the house consciously disengages from the ground, allowing the wind, quite literally, to blow sand from the hair. One of the four primal elements is exchanged for another.

Such a visceral relationship with nature was a requirement in the brief. For their weekend home the clients wanted to escape from urban pressures and environmental conditions, and hoped for an architectural solution that would offer to reconnect them with nature. Importantly, this was not just to be a shelter to retreat and observe, but to convey the physical force of the

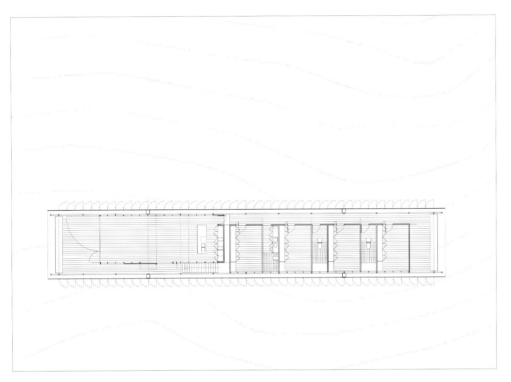

Left: **McNair House, Mornington Peninsula, Victoria, Australia.** Plan of the main level: the large living room opens onto a large terrace and faces the sea, while a smaller terrace off the guest bedroom at the other end gives a landside prospect

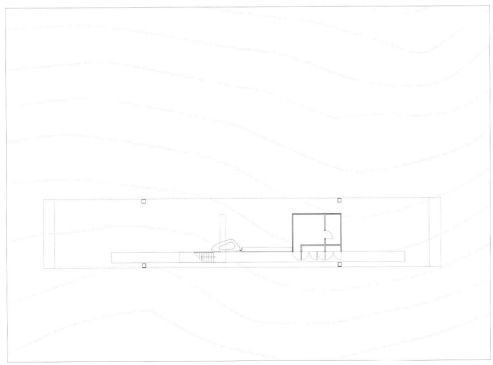

Left: **McNair House, Mornington Peninsula, Victoria, Australia.** Plan of the ground level: though a powerful formal statement in the landscape, its contact with the ground itself is minimal

elements after spending the working week in a homogenised 22-degree environment. That added some spice to the relatively ordinary needs for accommodation: a living area with three bedrooms for parents and children, and a separate guest suite. So all the individual spaces are connected not by an internal corridor, but by an outdoor promenade; to move from one room to another is to be exposed to the unmediated climate in all its extremes. Using architecture to 're-humanise' its occupants in this way is a counterpart to projects like Park Bench and Future Shack, which in a sense address the process of re-humanising at the other end of the socio-economic spectrum. What they do together is to suggest how architecture can help to assert a shared concept of humanity.

One of Godsell's skills as an architect is to match quite fundamental intellectual programmes with an ability to devise simple but sophisticated constructions, using elemental materials with careful detailing to bring out their character. Such skill is very evident in this house. Its shape intensifies the relationship to the sea and wind, while its skin, which might initially appear closed and protective, is largely of oxidised steel panels that can open up like brises-soleils as if allowing the house to breathe. Both conditions reflect the two cycles of weather and periodic occupation. Raising the house on columns allows land and air to flow beneath it – as well as providing ample storage and covered parking. The main living area, itself more than 10 metres long, focuses only in one direction, and a covered deck at its end seems to be an implicit invitation to move forward and sit outside, even in extreme conditions. Running along the length rather than across the width of the house, the staircase also reinforces its strong directionality. The bedrooms too are lined up in a serried rank behind, though the promenade does open the house to the side. Only with the fourth bedroom with its own deck, at the rear, does the house offer a distinctly different prospect.

In a subtle way, explains Godsell, the design of this house has added to his own understanding of history. It is the first design in which he has consciously inscribed a powerful geometry into the site in the manner of a French chateau, rather than nurturing its own apparently naturalistic setting in the manner of English landscape gardening, and this alternative approach seemed to come naturally from the site and programme. It certainly shows that architecture can engage with nature in many different ways, and that perhaps so strong a statement is a more appropriate way of reminding humans of their own frailty in the face of natural forces, as the clients wanted. As the painter Nicolas Poussin, himself one of the greatest French thinkers about landscape, might have said, "*Et in Arcadia ego*".

Right: **McNair House, Mornington Peninsula, Victoria, Australia.** Elevations: given the length of the cantilevers and the minimal structural supports, the side walls also act as trusses

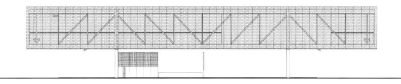

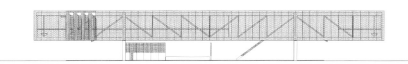

Opposite: **McNair House, Mornington Peninsula, Victoria, Australia.** The cantilever on the landside is similar to the one looking towards the sea and ends in an open terrace with a built-in bench in place of the traditional balustrade

Below: **McNair House, Mornington Peninsula, Victoria, Australia.** Rather than a corridor, the house has an outside deck to connect the different rooms

Below: **McNair House, Mornington Peninsula, Victoria, Australia.** The view from the living room terrace towards the ocean

House on Corfu

Timothy Hatton Architects
Corfu, Greece   2006

At one point along its east coast Corfu almost touches the Balkan mainland, but as if deliberately shunning such a connection, the island draws itself up to its full height, leaving a distance of just over a mile to Albania and giving itself a wonderful coastline of steep cliffs projecting and rising between small, sheltered coves. Despite its rugged appearance it has a long history of human adaptation and use. Affording safe shelter and abundant fresh water, the island once attracted merchant seafarers on their way between Italy, Constantinople and the Levant, much as today its physical beauty and relationship with the sea appeal to modern holidaymakers. By refining local architectural tradition to allow just enough latent history into the experience without overwhelming visitors, Tim Hatton's design captures the potential of this enviable landscape to provide respite from the stresses of contemporary life.

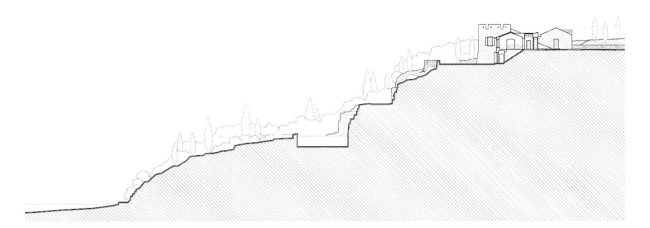

Above: **House on Corfu, Greece.** Site section. The house enjoys a commanding position but appears modest, especially from the land. In front of it is a vast terrace and, some way below, a large swimming pool is cut into the contours

Opposite: **House on Corfu, Greece.** The house has a magnificent site on a steeply sloping coast looking towards the mainland

Educated at Cambridge and Harvard, Hatton is at heart a Modernist but he infuses his designs with a sensibility that assimilates history and tradition. In this instance, the client suggested a starting point for the design which is more literal than Hatton would usually take. Already owning a nearby house where simplified Portuguese Baroque trimmings augment the basic but well-proportioned volume of an old olive press into a large house capable of accommodating many guests, the client felt a need for a more private retreat on another part of the property. He selected a site with a commanding position overlooking the narrow sea channel and enjoying distant views into Albania, where an estuarine plain dominated by a perfectly formed volcanic cone lies between ranges of hills. For such a position, there was an obvious precedent in the type of watchtower to be found all along Corfu's coast. Its appeal lay in its being a small, freestanding building where he could have a bedroom on an upper level, and leave the uses of the remaining accommodation to emerge in due course.

Typically only two storeys high, these watchtowers are short and can appear somewhat squat, though their volume and construction from local stone give them an affinity with vernacular structures, olive presses being a common example. Chamfered lower walls implying greater strength at the base, however, and especially their castellated tops leave no doubt as to their defensive purpose. This combined origin in vernacular and military architecture was an appropriate starting point because of its explicit connections to local character and Corfu's history. It offered the opportunity to bypass civil architecture with its potential for sophisticated cultural references, and instead to devise an architectural idiom from more basic principles. A watchtower may not have been Hatton's first choice for a precedent, but it has a logic: it offered the opportunity for a design to develop from the locality and its past without obvious or overt reference to the overlaid stimuli of modern existence, and as such was well suited to the house's purpose as a retreat.

As Hatton started to work out how to adapt the watchtower form into a comfortable bedroom the client began to soften. It was slightly unfair, he realised, to leave his wife languishing amid Portuguese Baroque trimming when he was enjoying a view from his solid, unadorned tower, and so a bedroom and bathroom for her were incorporated into the design. As the tower now had a side extension it lost its formal perfection and almost begged for compositional balance. Meanwhile the client, too, recognised that he needed more than just a bedroom on this part of the property, and in asking Hatton to add a study suggested a way of improving the ensemble. But it was to be a study without benefit of the view – that would be too diverting from serious work. That meant the logical place for it was just above the second bedroom, turning itself into the rock and lit by dormer windows in the double-pitched roof. Though entirely new, its volume and construction, dormers aside, recall the olive press drawing room in the original house.

Above: **House on Corfu, Greece.** An outside staircase leads to the tower roof

Left: **House on Corfu, Greece.** Plan: the solid construction gives each of the rooms and volumes a strong physical presence

Right: **House on Corfu, Greece.** Elevation from the sea, facing east – acquiring a second tower balances the composition

Above: **House on Corfu, Greece.** A sturdy retaining wall defines the precinct for the house and encloses a generous terrace paved with giant slabs

Left: **House on Corfu, Greece.** The use of traditional building crafts and materials gives the house a timeless feel

As the house grew its circulation acquired a complexity that buildings with one or two rooms do not have, which was not made any easier by the steeply sloping site. But Hatton turned this to advantage, running an outside staircase up to the roof of the tower, and dropping a flight of steps from the study, first to a half landing where another flight connecting the bedrooms runs across it at right angles, before continuing to a room in the tower's base.

With a small fountain at its centre and a portrait of Ali Pasha on one wall, it is a place for reverie, though leaving it for the bright light of the terrace outside would dispel any daydream.

After some seasons of using his new study, the client softened again. It was a shame, he felt, that he and his wife could have no guests in their new retreat. Hatton, realising that the composition could still benefit from a little more anchorage, suggested a second tower joined to the first by a two-storey range, which could have a huge bath- and exercise room on the first floor, together with a kitchen and dining room leading directly on to the terrace. The new tower would contain another bedroom suite.

Having grown so much, the house has horizontal presence on the cliffside which the original concept of a single tower could never have had. Viewed from the sea it is clearly not a simple watchtower but a substantial edifice, though from the landside – where the approach is from above – it still appears to be a modest, single-storey structure as the lower floor is concealed by the slope. It could just be a complex of agricultural buildings, though Hatton has contrived a small courtyard in the right angle between the entrance to the study and the range between the two towers. The cool and spatial qualities of the study, the commanding presence of the main bedroom and the wry fantasy of the fountain room remain hidden.

Left: **House on Corfu, Greece.** A study without a view: its generous dimensions and elegant proportions make it a congenial place to work without distraction

Writing with Light House

Steven Holl
Eastern Long Island, New York, USA   2004

Steven Holl's intellectual explorations frequently reach far beyond architecture's conventional boundaries. In an early house he turned to that old favourite, the intervals of the musical scale, though the design that resulted was anything but classical, while a more recent office building in Amsterdam explored the potential for interaction between a 'Menger sponge' and Morton Feldman's composition *Patterns in a Chromatic Field*. Always there is a fascination with light – as a functional tool, in its susceptibility to colour and for its symbolic potential. His Jesuit Chapel at Seattle University dating from the mid 1990s notionally decanted light into seven stone 'bottles'. Combining sensory impressions and intellectual concepts in a symbolic representation of Catholic theology and the Jesuit mission, the building's overt programme gives structure and meaning to light's purely elemental and visual effects.

As its name suggests, Writing with Light House uses the same phenomenon but, as its function also implies, to a different purpose. And where the Jesuit Chapel had an agenda that would have been the same in Sydney or Singapore as in Seattle, for this house Holl looked for a point of departure that had some connection to its location on Long Island. It came from the coincidental proximity of Jackson Pollock's studio, and his 1945 painting *There Were Seven in Eight* made the starting point for several free-form design sketches. Through them the idea of 'writing with light' emerged. Holl elaborated the idea, as he often does in his design process, with a series of paintings that move from the abstraction of Pollock to an increasingly literal

Above: **Writing with Light House, Long Island, New York, USA.** Holl explored the idea of 'writing with light' in a series of sketches and paintings that relate abstract concepts to material conditions

Left: **Writing with Light House, Long Island, New York, USA.** In this painting Holl investigates the interaction between light, surface, volume and view

Above: **Writing with Light House, Long Island, New York, USA.** The south elevation of horizontally laid timber strips makes a ghostly screen for the formal and spatial dynamics behind

representation of an architectural language. Through this exploratory process the idea that light could become instrumental, investigative and even instructive emerged, adapting inert matter and vacant space to its will, the paintings initially exploring and then demonstrating the particular effects he wanted. As Holl wrote on one sketch, "Linear strips of sunlight inscribe and bend internal spaces dynamically in time". Though painting rather than theology, mathematics or music is the starting point as well as the design method for this project, it is through reinterpretation in his own paintings that Holl's interest in light and time is introduced into the house.

The site has a more literal influence on the design than the paintings of a long-dead artist who happened to have a studio nearby. In this flat and sandy landscape, water is the most attractive feature, and as an inlet forms the site's northern edge, it determines the house's orientation in that direction. Across this relatively narrow stretch of water are more dunes, the odd house and a more distant view to the ocean itself, visible from the first-floor level. As the house opens up to the north, so the south has to be closed to provide

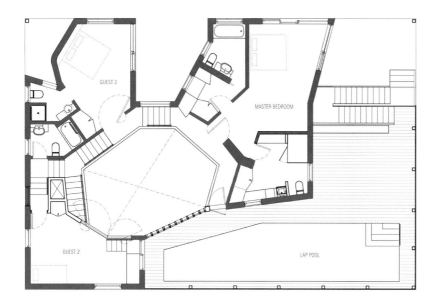

Left: **Writing with Light House, Long Island, New York, USA.** First-floor plan: bedrooms spiral off the staircase at different heights

Above: **Writing with Light House, Long Island, New York, USA.** Ground-floor plan: Steven Holl has eroded a standard rectangle into a complex pattern of interlocking shapes and volumes in three dimensions

Below: **Writing with Light House, Long Island, New York, USA.** Site plan: to the north the site boundary is an inlet from the ocean

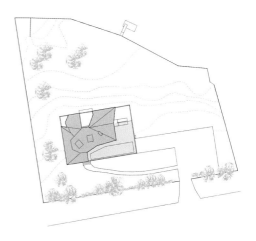

Above: **Writing with Light House, Long Island, New York, USA.** View from the dining room into the living room: each room is a clearly defined space and they interlock in a manner which might recall Adolf Loos' 'Raumplan'. But using function as his cue, Loos rarely departed from orthogonal geometries, whereas Holl, here using the idea of light, introduces the diagonal

privacy, and the two main facades reflect this distinction between them. The south facade, which contains the entrance, is essentially a uniform plane of horizontal timber strips. Though there are openings for door and windows, there is only a shadowy hint of volumetric gymnastics at first-floor level.

On the other side, to the north, the house quite literally opens up. The horizontal timber slats are there, but so is an expressed timber frame, defining a volume which includes a series of outdoor spaces such as a deck for looking towards the ocean on the upper storey, as well as the actual rooms. There are also traces of habitation and function like the staircase that connects the observation deck to a ground-level terrace. From this angle the house reveals two characteristics which are concealed from the entrance: it appropriates the traditional balloon frame construction of rural American dwellings, but it is also clearly coerced into a volumetric and spatial composition of unusual complexity. Not until the interior, however, are the full extent and nature of that complexity revealed, and a deeper purpose to the contrasting treatment of the facades becomes apparent.

Even the seemingly plain entrance front conceals a surprise. The front door is not on axis with the short flight of steps leading to a small porch but positioned to the left. It opens into a lobby and orients visitors away from the main living room to give it some privacy, though this simple device also introduces a sense of spiralling movement through space. Turning from the entrance towards the living room brings a staircase into view that branches into two loose spirals leading upwards in the opposite directions to three of the four bedrooms and, in one case, the observation deck which has a small lap pool against the entrance facade.

In the living room the complexities multiply further. Reaching the full height of the house, it is irregular in both plan and section, and as if that were not enough it seems to extend into other only partly concealed spaces: a library, a dining room and a sheltered terrace. But overwhelming all the other architectural devices are the effects of light. Strips of sunlight penetrate the gaps between the timber slats on the entrance facade and end up on the floor. Smoother light emanates from high-level windows and wafts down the walls. Internal angles and projections introduce their own patterns of shadow onto any of the variegated surfaces that will accept them. There are even some views to the outside.

The strange interaction of these contrasting effects might be analogous to the intense introspection of Pollock's paintings. But the medium here is light and the precision with which its effects are orchestrated might have a parallel in writing. It certainly establishes the terms on which the spaces, textures and forms are seen. Holl's approach to architecture is unashamedly cerebral and his intellectual programmes are more explicit than those of most architects who strive for the same status. For many the interaction between constraints of brief and site is enough to generate a design, but Holl always seeks to introduce another element to the programme, which serves to triangulate what can become a rather dull iteration. If the introduction here of painting, and its transformation into 'writing with light' may seem to dilute the relationship between place and people that characterises most houses in the country, it also serves to show how architecture can address landscapes of the inner mind as well as the outer world.

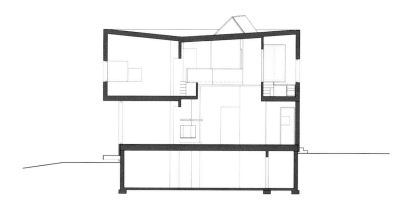

Left: **Writing with Light House, Long Island, New York, USA.** Section through the library and entrance hall, looking east *(left)* and a long section through the living room and kitchen, looking north *(below)*

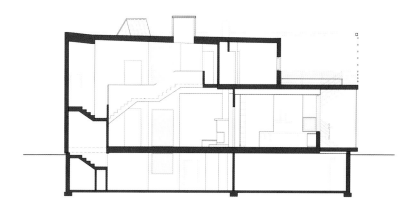

Opposite: **Writing with Light House, Long Island, New York, USA.** Light is always there: what turns it into writing are the apertures to give it shape, and the solid surfaces to catch it

Dirk Cove

Niall McLaughlin
Dirk Cove, County Cork, Ireland   2005

Whether its intricate and angular forms seem to mesh with the rocky shards of Ireland's west coast, or it appears as a focus for the light of a dawn halo, Niall McLaughlin's remodelling of a coastguard's cottage engages in an interaction with its surroundings which is every bit as complex as their forms and the traditions with which they have become interwoven. The jagged coastline evokes tortured relationships between the land's anguished history and the turbulent ocean, but with the possibility of catharsis which echoes one that Seamus Heaney indicated in *Lovers on Aran*:

Above: **Dirk Cove, County Cork, Ireland.** The house grows out of a former coastguard station, its materials proclaiming its newness, its forms reflecting its natural setting

> *Did sea define the land or land the sea?*
> *Each drew new meaning from the waves' collision.*
> *Sea broke on land to full identity.*

Appearing to evolve from the natural and artificial forms already on the site, and in its orientation towards the sea, McLaughlin uses architecture to explore those potential meanings.

The house's original purpose had a strong bearing on its position, siting and construction, while its role as part of the machinery of British occupation in Ireland, albeit a small and relatively benign one, influenced its subsequent history. It lies at the end of the road: here land transport yielded to boats, and as those boats had to be launched in rough weather, the location of the house

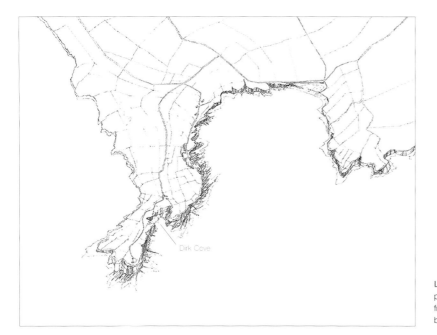

Left: **Dirk Cove, County Cork, Ireland.** Site plan: the original slipway took advantage of shelter from the prevailing south-westerly weather so that boats could be launched in storms

Above: **Dirk Cove, County Cork, Ireland.** The expansive Modernist composition seems to invite a dialogue with nature

and in particular the angle of the slipway take advantage of the natural cove, which gives some protection from prevailing south-westerly storms. The cottage itself, perhaps because its occupants had regularly to dice with death at sea, turns its back on the water, while its construction follows the vernacular convention of small windows and thick walls, so precluding easy connections between exterior and interior. But in the troubled period of the early 1920s, which saw the establishment of an independent Irish state, that mattered little. The coastguard's station fell into disrepair and with resources for public services greatly stretched in the new and poverty-stricken country, it remained so, its brickwork and masonry gradually sinking into ruinous romance.

With social and economic progress those picturesque attractions began to overcome the legacy of history. By the early twenty-first century, Ireland surpassed its former master in per capita affluence and, for the first time in centuries, attracted immigrants from its diasporous communities. Under these circumstances a dramatic and isolated site of great beauty became an attractive proposition. Not far from Cork and its airport, it could be reached

relatively easily by people living outside Ireland, but who wanted an accessible retreat. The challenge was to find an architecture that would draw out its inherent beauties without overwhelming its historic and natural significance.

McLaughlin is known for seductive and flamboyant forms, but certainly their seductiveness and perhaps their flamboyance are heightened by an extraordinary sensibility to the existing qualities of place. It might have been easy, in this landscape, to erase the traces of human occupation and start again by creating a direct relationship between nature and artifice. But instead McLaughlin re-used the old cottage, recognising that its construction, orientation and form possessed qualities that were appropriate for some of the activities in the new house. Consequently, it was remodelled to provide a bedroom and bathroom suite, while its simple orthogonal geometry helped to position the garage and entrance, and also suggested a discreet and protected location for guest accommodation. McLaughlin describes the composition as a "relatively lazy crucifix", and this easy relationship seems to have found a counterpart in a sympathetic county architect who was relaxed about the prospect of a contemporary building on this precious section of Ireland's southern coast.

The homely, comforting buildings with their vernacular origins make an appropriate sounding board for the most dramatic new element, the sharded

Above: **Dirk Cove, County Cork, Ireland.**
"There is no such thing as bad weather," Ruskin said, "only different types of good weather ... " Shortly after completion Dirk Cove survived the worst storm in 100 years, when stones and seaweed were thrown onto the roof

Opposite: **Dirk Cove, County Cork, Ireland.**
Plan: the new extension has some affinity with the dagger-like shards of rock which project into the sea

Below: **Dirk Cove, County Cork, Ireland.**
Section through the old coastguard's cottage,
with the new extension in elevation

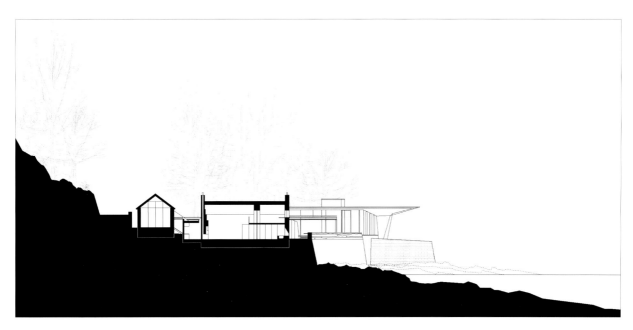

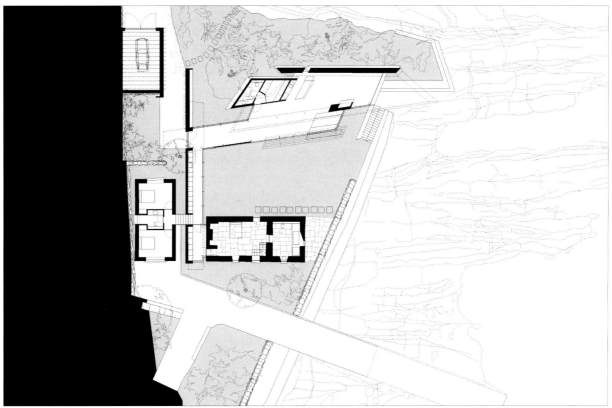

and faceted living space. Visible from a distance, it disappears behind a thick wall, which is parallel though staggered with the garage. Penetrating it through the entrance reveals each of the elements, but in a new relationship to one another. Ahead is the living space, a mass of light, shadow, frames, planes and cantilevers; to the right is the old cottage. Between the two is the closest such a site can have to a formal lawn, held in position by the sea wall. Ahead, framed by the old and new buildings, is the ocean – uncontrollable, unfathomable, but rendered through a carefully contrived frame.

In this context the powerful forms of the living area are fully appropriate. They might take their cue from the angular fingers of rock, dark and menacing, that penetrate the sea. If so, they mediate their elemental qualities into the finished materials of steel, glass and white render, while each angle and plane inflects the gaze towards a particular object or vista. This space turns the intense duel between land and sea into a delicate cat's cradle of light, reflection and shadow, turning and transforming into spatial qualities what nature left as purely volumetric. Rendering nature into ephemeral space with an almost narrative-like ability to unfold over time merges with levels of comfort, such as the seats and fireplace, to make the room both congenial and stimulating. The sea can soothe or threaten; but here its dangers are turned into an aesthetic and emotional condition, recalling Ruskin's dictum that "there is no such thing as bad weather, only different types of good weather". As if to prove the point, shortly after completion the house withstood the full force of the fiercest storm for 100 years, sustaining no noticeable damage despite stones being hurled onto the lawn and seaweed onto the roof.

The house transforms McLaughlin's compositional 'lazy crucifix' into a symbolic one. Between the intimacy of a retreat and the openness that such a site invites is a powerful axis, while a weaker or more sinuous one runs across it, joining history and its traditions to conditions laid down by nature. It is the interaction between them that allows the restrictions of each pole to be transcended, opening the eyes to what lies beyond the limits of immediate perceptions, as Seamus Heaney hinted:

> The timeless waves, bright sifting, broken glass
> Came dazzling around, into the rocks,
> Came glinting, sifting from the Americas.

Below: **Dirk Cove, County Cork, Ireland.** The
house at dusk, the sun setting to the west on the
far side of the peninsula

Beach House

Lacaton Vassal

Keremma, Brittany, France   2005

Ever since they chose the site for a traditional wattle-and-stick house in the desert of Niger in the early 1980s, Anne Lacaton and Jean-Philippe Vassal have been fascinated by the challenge of making a home from almost nothing other than imagination and its interaction with the qualities of a site. The house in Niger was no more than a circular wattle wall, enclosing a simple domed hut and adjoining a rectangular wattle roof resting on nine posts, all resting on a sand bank. Their celebrated house at Cap Ferret near Bordeaux (1998), embracing a tree on a wooded sand dune, shows how building on sand remained a feature of their work when they returned to France, even as they began to explore the aesthetic and volumetric possibilities of industrially produced components. This house at Keremma, near Roscoff on the northern coast of Brittany, continues the same theme.

Its site has the typical qualities of a sandy seafront. Two strips run between dry land and sea, one pure beach and the other a protective sand dune stabilised by vegetation. All this occupies only a few dozen metres but the dune, though low, is high enough to conceal the sea from the site. Instead, it makes its presence felt via the sound of waves breaking on the beach. In this interstitial zone between the sea and firm ground, where biblical lore suggests a house should be built, visibility is not enough: the site's true character only becomes apparent when all the senses combine to stimulate the imagination. Conventional perceptions dissolve in such conditions, and new possibilities take their place.

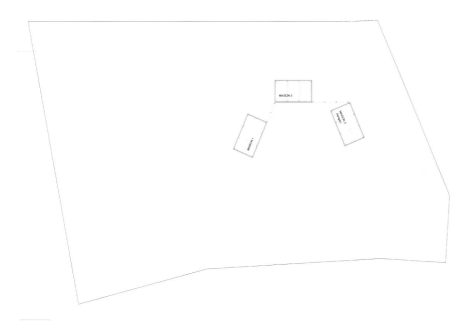

Left: **Beach House, Keremma, Brittany, France.** Site plan: the grouping of the three volumes is just off symmetrical, and the position of the open shutters reinforces the dynamic balance between them

Above: **Beach House, Keremma, Brittany, France.** View from the 'hangar': when the house is in use the corrugated-metal 'shutters' slide out to become screens enclosing a large outdoor space

To Lacaton these very particular qualities of nature are never entirely benign, and architecture is the discipline that adapts them to human use. Whether on the edge of desert or ocean, architecture starts by using what shelter occurs naturally and adding whatever is necessary to tame but not exclude the elements. Here the house, divided into three separated volumes, is pushed to the northern and eastern limits of the site, where a group of trees affords some protection. This arrangement presents a convex face to the north, defending the precinct from inclement weather, while offering a concave face to the south to create an intimate and protected exterior space which receives the southern sun. Occupation of the house emphasises this particular characteristic. When empty the three volumes are solid and separated, but when the house is inhabited the walls slide open, linking the three parts into a single curving sun trap, with minimal barriers dividing the interior spaces from the outdoor court.

All three blocks have the same dimensions of 13 x 7.6 metres on plan with a double pitched roof 5.6 metres high, producing a volume not dissimilar

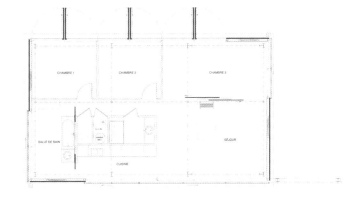

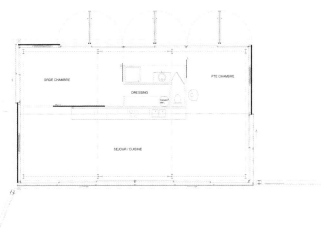

Right: **Beach House, Keremma, Brittany, France.** Plans: the western block *(right)* has a series of enclosed spaces and can function as a self-contained guest house. The main block *(below)* is a single volume, open to the roof, though it can be divided by sliding partitions

to the image of a house that a child might draw. What keeps this reference at an abstract level, however, and provides one means of differentiating the blocks from each other, is the choice of cladding. Other means of expressing the blocks' differences are their internal organisation and manner of closing. If it were not for the artful positioning and careful detailing, these three volumes might be mistaken for a trio of basic barns, individually adapted to particular needs. Each has its own internal character and a particular relationship with the exterior, which follows logically from that character.

At some subliminal level the overall composition might have some reference to the traditional *parti* of a main block flanked by a pair of wings around a *cour d'honneur*, and in keeping with this the central volume is the heart of the complex. A living room-cum-kitchen occupies almost the entire volume up to the roof, though a pair of sliding screens can divide two sleeping spaces adjacent to the bathroom according to the number of occupants. Solid walls slide back to reveal the interiors and from most of the interior one is aware of the total volume, though from the outside glass screens interrupt and reflect some views, creating a richness of transparency and opacity that responds to the human need for occasional privacy as well as a sense of depth and space. In a landscape where sound, wind and smell seem to merge and to roll like low clouds over the topography and between the foliage, the house begins to imply if not impose a sense of structure and order that complements nature's own structure of the dune as means of protecting land from sea. Here nature and architectural space interact, not in opposition but changing each other's natures in a continuous flow.

The second building, to the west, is divided into smaller spaces. Inserted into the roof is a floor with five or six beds for children, while at ground level are a living room, a kitchen, three large bedrooms and a large bathroom. As a logical extension of dividing the volume into smaller, defined spaces, every room has a particular character, and this is reinforced by giving each its own unique view to the outside. Reflecting the division of the inside, the relationship between interior and exterior is treated as a series of discrete events.

Most fluid of all in function and in its lack of distinction between inside and out is the third block, to the east. The architects describe it as a 'hangar', a large shed clad in transparent polycarbonate. Apart from an opaque enclosure with a shower and storage space it is entirely open, and the floor is compacted sand like the ground outside – a device that emphasises its ambiguous status between inside and out. With this floor the architects suggest that the block is outdoors without the inconveniences, especially when its walls open to allow the continuity of ground surface to become apparent and only the vertical posts interrupt the flow of people and air. Here, games can be played when it rains, hammocks can be set up for summer nights, meals served on sunny winter days and plants placed for protection from frost. The building is a graphic illustration of Lacaton's characterisation of architecture as the means to make nature habitable, but not to exclude it. As well as responding to nature, it also responds to the various strands in family life; its division means that it can be occupied by a couple, with or without children, grand-children and guests; different generations can entertain themselves without disturbing each other, but always aware of a ghostly presence – the sea.

HANGAR

RESERVE

PLAN

House in Dorset

Nigel Anderson of **Robert Adam Architects**
North Dorset, UK   2003

Despite challenges from the Picturesque, Gothic Revival, Arts and Crafts and even Modernism, classical architecture has always been a strong element in the idea of the English country house. From the grandest intellectual conceptions of Lord Burlington and his protégés to small manor houses where a simplified pair of half columns and pediment surround the entrance, classicism has proved versatile enough to adapt to different budgets, to absorb local building traditions and materials, and to become sufficiently widespread to turn it into one of the touchstones of the English ruling classes' identity and cohesion. Classicism is also what remains as the other reasons for identity and cohesion dissolve, so it is no surprise that classical country house building continues, albeit in several different forms.

One of the most prolific exponents of this particular architectural genre is Robert Adam Architects. They have built over 50 rural houses across the UK and the majority are classical in affiliation. Some are ineffably grand attempts to recreate ducal residences; others, such as this example in the south coast county of Dorset, are modest and develop the thread typified by masons such as the Bastard family of Blandford in the same county, who gradually absorbed enough classical lore to produce designs which are recognisably in the tradition. In this flexible and undogmatic approach Adam and his firm echo the slow and evolutionary way classicism became part of British architecture, but also stand apart from fellow contemporary neo-classicists, who are inclined to view classical architecture as a strict canon which may have divine authority. The firm's pragmatism leads it to welcome

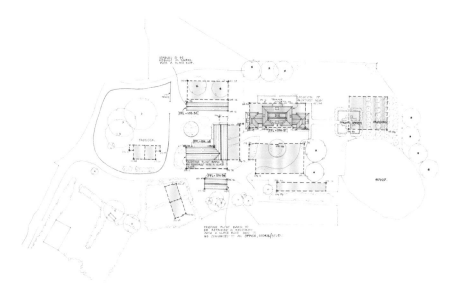

Left: House in Dorset, North Dorset, UK.
Site plan, showing the demolished agricultural buildings in pink, the new house in purple and the refurbished barns in blue

Above: **House in Dorset, North Dorset, UK.**
Anderson's intention was to recreate the free
classicism of the very early eighteenth century

modern technology and allows it to cater for specific programmatic
requirements. As other architects have found, sconces and scrolls are ideal
for concealing the wiring that can so easily compromise minimalism.

Nigel Anderson, the director responsible for this house, has a particular
liking for the architecture of gentle, smaller-scale, eighteenth-century English
houses and a compatible penchant for the more inventive among Arts and
Crafts house plans, matching an aesthetic pragmatism with a functional one.
Here, the client particularly wanted the building to convey an impression of
the early eighteenth century, just before Burlington and his circle codified a
Neo-Palladian canon. Ideally, he says, it would have been constructed from
one of the local stones, which are soft to work and warm to the touch, though
there are historical precedents for the rendered finish that was chosen and
which, at a comparable price to a good quality facing brick, is significantly
cheaper. Its classical allusions are just as obvious, first in the symmetry and

Left: **House in Dorset, North Dorset, UK.** Side elevation: classical detail, though sparse, evokes the whole panoply of the period

Below: **House in Dorset, North Dorset, UK.** Entrance elevation: two lower wings flank a three-storey main block

Above: **House in Dorset, North Dorset, UK.**
The house sits in the north Dorset plain

second in the relatively sparse but easily recognisable classical detail. The pitched roof confirms the principal inspiration as early eighteenth century; within a decade or two the Palladian Revival had abolished the pitch and brought in the parapet and balustrade.

The symmetrical composition also closely follows the same precedents. The central block has seven bays, with the outer pair at each end standing slightly forward from the recessed central three, with the entrance in the middle. This convention is perhaps a memory of an even older period where two wings projected to form an entrance courtyard, though in the models for this house a courtyard had become strictly vestigial. Again, the Palladian Revival tended to render the entrance facade, at least that of the main block, as a flat plane; if anything stood forward, it was the entrance itself, preferably as a portico, though in smaller houses a porch might suffice. One feature of this house that might owe just a fraction to the Palladian Revival are the wings.

In Palladio's villas the wings housed working farms. By the time the concept reached England the scale, grandeur and ambition increased: houses like Holkham and Kedleston Halls use wings to enhance their presence and aura within their settings. But wings also served a practical purpose. They were one way of adding accommodation without the need to incur the expense of building a full second storey, and for this reason Palladian wings sometimes grew out of existing houses. The pair Capability Brown added to the little-known Beechwood Park in Hertfordshire, then a very early eighteenth-century facade under a pitched roof (itself concealing a house of Tudor origins), are a good example. In other examples they could house new or expanded functions, such as ballrooms or libraries. At this house, at the smaller end of the scale, the wings still serve the same purpose, one housing a billiard room, the other serving as a utility room and office.

The classical ornament is sparse, but rather than being spread thinly across the whole building, it is concentrated in particular places, partly to indicate their relative importance and partly to provide elements of unambiguous Classicism, so leaving the imagination to fill in the gaps. Robert Adam himself argues that a mere hint of correct classical detail, provided the proportions and massing are in keeping, is enough to stimulate the mind to infer the whole panoply of decoration. In this house, the entrance porch, cornice and side door into the kitchen wing assume that role.

Opposite: **House in Dorset, North Dorset, UK.**
Rear elevation: apart from the fenestration of the wings, the house is symmetrical

The plan follows the exterior's straightforward logic. A central entrance leads to a triple-height hall capped, at the particular request of the client, with a lantern, and faced with a three-leg staircase. On axis and projecting in a central bay on the garden front is a formal dining room; on either side of the hall are the drawing room and kitchen, with a small sitting room beyond. The wings provide another flanking layer.

In its unfussy way, the plan illustrates what Anderson characterises as the common expectations in a house such as this. "The core of the house," he says, "are the everyday activities of living, cooking and eating." Even houses with servants have no equivalent of the green baize door that separated their zone from their employer's. Nowadays, everyone wants to

Below: **House in Dorset, North Dorset, UK.**
Built in what was a farmyard, the house does not have an established park and its immediate surroundings are currently sparsely planted

show off their kitchen and culinary skills, and though they may want an Aga that resembles a nineteenth-century cooking range, they would not be without their electric hobs and microwaves. Against this backdrop Anderson also notes the re-emergence of a modern equivalent of the Victorian front parlour, a room only entered on special occasions. In this house, it is the billiard room, accessible only through the drawing room. Though these two rooms were *de rigueur* in any respectable country house of the late nineteenth century, this arrangement would have had Victorian bachelors who played billiards and their dowager aunts who ruled the drawing room spinning equally quickly in their graves; it was not just servants and gentry whom Victorian architects had to separate, but genders and generations.

In the late seventeenth and early eighteenth centuries, modest country houses tended to be situated on the edge of or very close to existing settlements, and their surroundings would have been mature and lush. They were an integral part of the ordering of the landscape into a pattern which reflected the social hierarchy. The relationship between this house and its setting is very different. There is no village. Though it does have a small estate, at only 200 acres it is not large enough to support a house of this size. Instead, it provides facilities for rural leisure, riding and shooting, expensive pursuits which require resources from urbanised economies to operate. The purpose of the existing farm buildings, too, was not to run a farm – they had long since outlived that purpose. Instead, in line with the rigid planning policy for rural building in the UK, they were to be treated as ugly eyesores deserving replacement. So what underpins the reproduction of early eighteenth-century architecture is a mature and sophisticated economy, filtered through the politically controlled planning system, which itself favours nostalgia. In this sense, more than ever, classicism provides the continuity.

Right: **House in Dorset, North Dorset, UK.**
Though still the heart of a working farm, the
house is larger than anything but a large estate
could maintain

Left: **House in Dorset, North Dorset, UK.**
First-floor plan: symmetry adjusted to meet
modern expectations

Left: **House in Dorset, North Dorset, UK.**
Ground-floor plan. In the modern country
house, the kitchen has become the most
inhabited room, while the billiard room is
only used for special occasions

Slefringe Herrgård

Mikael Bergquist
Östergötland, Sweden   2003

Slefringe Herrgård is typical of the modest manor houses that the Swedish aristocracy built from the seventeenth century onwards. Until the early eighteenth century the country was a major European power, and its architecture was continually invigorated by an influx of ideas and practitioners from the south. But the nobles lacked the resources of their French and British counterparts, and though houses like Slefringe are recognisably part of the classical tradition, they tend to be greatly simplified and adapted to the limited capabilities of the local construction industry. Indeed, Slefringe itself was not much more than a farmhouse until extended in the 1920s. That ethos of simplicity and an ability to make the most of whatever skills are available is a connecting thread in Swedish architecture, from National Romanticism, through Neo-Classicism to Functionalism. It is also traceable in Mikael Bergquist's swimming pool extension at Slefringe Herrgård, making the building a modest representative of more than one period of Swedish country house design.

Slefringe is in Östergötland, a province in the eastern part of the country, south of Stockholm. It is near a small town called Åtvidaberg and a little way to the south of the two larger centres of Linköping and Norrköping. The landscape in this part of Sweden rolls gently across a vast territory, with

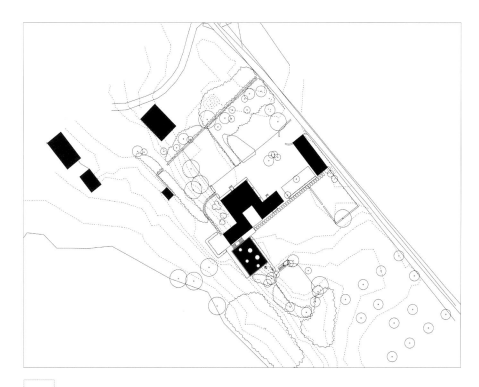

Left: **Slefringe Herrgård, Östergötland, Sweden.**
Site plan: the site slopes gently up from a lake

Above: **Slefringe Herrgård, Östergötland, Sweden.** The new pool house takes advantage of the view over the water

lakes forming in shallow valleys with thick forest around them. On this natural scenery the small towns and occasional nobleman's seat make only local impact. The house sits on a cleared gentle slope just above a lake. The oldest parts date from the seventeenth century, and the principal block is rectangular with a traditional layout of six rooms. The two wings built on in the 1920s formed a small courtyard to the rear, added accommodation and gave the house slightly more presence in the landscape. They may have been designed by Isak Gustaf Clason, whose most famous work is a National Romantic extravaganza, the Nordic Museum in Stockholm (1889-1907), since he also redesigned Adelsnäs Castle, the principal seat of the family that still owns Slefringe today. The garden at Slefringe dates from the same period and was definitely designed by the landscape architect Rudolf Abelin.

Left: **Slefringe Herrgård, Östrergötland, Sweden.** Sweden entices in summertime

Above: **Slefringe Herrgård, Östrergötland, Sweden.** Rear elevation of the original house, with the pool house in section

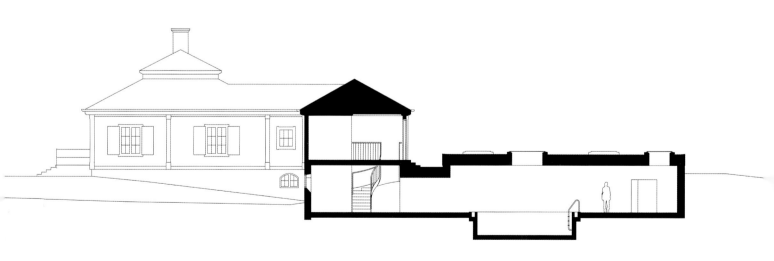

Above: **Slefringe Herrgård, Östrergötland, Sweden.** The two wings nearest the camera were added to the original manor house in the 1920s, forming a small courtyard between them

Opposite: **Slefringe Herrgård, Östrergötland, Sweden.** Long section through pool house, with one side of the original house in elevation

Bergquist's clients, the current baron and baroness, provide the link between the two houses. Having lived in the castle, when they reached their 60s they wanted something smaller and more manageable, as so many do these days, and the so-called 'dolls' manor' at Slefringe seemed the obvious solution. But it was in a sorry state after a brutal renovation in the 1960s, and turning it into their new home would necessarily combine outright restoration with a remodelling of the grounds, in addition to their wish for a new pool house. The baron and baroness were keen to create a contemporary but contextual design, and decided that the task should go to a young architect; Mikael Bergquist was recommended to them via a landscape architect with whom he had worked.

Though he designs in a contemporary idiom, Bergquist infuses his work with a deep understanding of Swedish architectural history. He appreciates the congenial idiosyncrasies of its domestic planning, and has made a particular study of the work of Josef Frank, the Austrian architect who contributed a pair of subtle houses, deceptive in their simplicity, to the *Weissenhofseidlung* in Stuttgart before taking refuge from the Nazis in Sweden. There, he found fertile ground for channelling his flair for inventive domestic design into several houses and rather more fabrics and furniture for the Svenska Tenn company. But Bergquist also has a sense for the near Brutalist intensity of expression of such architects as Sigurd Lewerentz and Peter Celsing. At Slefringe Herrgård both aspects are present, the first in the restoration of the house and the second in the pool house. Bergquist's task as a designer was to bring them together in a landscape that is so typical of Sweden you almost expect to see Ingmar Bergman's devil striding in for a game of chess.

In form, position and material the pool house clearly differs from the main building. It breaks the symmetry; its finish, *in situ* concrete, is untreated and it is folded into an existing terrace in the ground so that it engages with the landscape without either becoming subsumed within or dominating it. The pool house is essentially one large, rectilinear space, with an adjoining changing room and lavatory in the basement of one of the wings. The relationship with the main house is subtle and multifaceted. At a practical level the connection is below ground; an external staircase runs between and clearly distinguishes them from one another. Its roof is grassed. On one side is the stone base of the house; on the other the exposed concrete of the pool house.

This finish belies the delicacy of the interior. Within these spaces is a series of circular or elliptical forms: several rooflights, a cylindrical sauna and the pool itself. The surfaces are exquisite, whether the blue-grey stone floor, the mirror-like finish of the water that is level with the floor, the stuccoed walls or the timber work of the sauna. A glazed wall to the south-west affords a picture-like view over the lake and its surrounding forested shores. In striving for delicacy through a carefully assembled and limited palette of materials and a clear relationship with nature, the pool house gives contemporary expression to a much older tradition of Swedish country houses.

That tradition is displayed in the main house. In its oldest part the original room layout has been recreated and some old wall paintings restored. Though simple, the rooms are elegantly proportioned, while carefully placed doors and windows enhance the sense of space, light and flow. Internally the wings have been remodelled, on one side to provide a large kitchen and ancillary spaces, and on the other a single large room. What Bergquist shows, through a sensitivity to various periods of Swedish architectural history and towards domestic life, is how a contemporary idiom can be added as a counterpoint to and enhancement of this traditional elegance.

Left: **Slefringe Herrgård, Östrergötland, Sweden.** A generic Swedish setting, but a very un-generic building, despite its knowing relationship to Swedish tradition

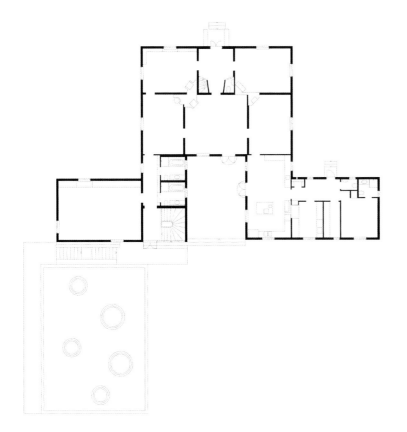

Above: **Slefringe Herrgård, Östergötland, Sweden.** Integrated simplicity: the sauna

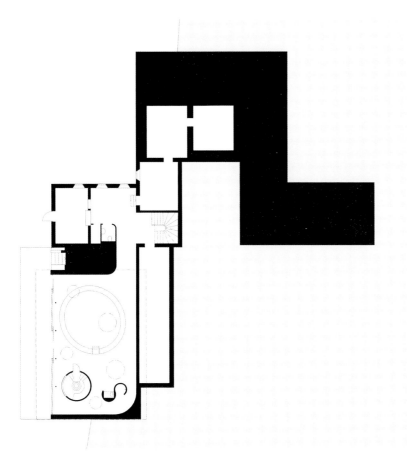

Left: **Slefringe Herrgård, Östergötland, Sweden.** Plan of the pool level: as well as the pool itself, the space includes an enclosed sauna and other semi-sculptural features

Below: **Slefringe Herrgård, Östrergötland, Sweden.** In keeping with Swedish tradition, the entry is modest and elaborated only with functional objects such as the benches

Du Plessis House

Marcio Kogan
near Paraty, Brazil   2003

Nature has favoured the coast between Rio de Janeiro and São Paolo with numerous attractions, so after half a millennium of European settlement and with a mega-city at either end, it is hardly surprising that humans have left their mark on the white beaches and the tropical rainforest in the not-too-distant hinterland. Marcio Kogan's Du Plessis House is a recent and particularly apt example of a design which acknowledges this history, but also looks towards a relationship with the landscape. The design explicitly combines tradition with modernity, and running like a helix through that relationship is the age-old architectural theme of nature and artifice.

One of the country's most compelling attractions was gold, which was discovered inland in Minas Gerais but transported to the coast for export to Portugal, the colonial power. That enterprise and the wealth it generated led to one of the most important human interventions on the coast, the historic city of Paraty which lies about 15 kilometres from the house. It became the second largest port in the country. The 'Gold Cycle', as the period of transitory prosperity came to be known, lasted long enough for two-storey houses to become the norm and churches to spawn a few extra layers of decoration, but not so long that its charming colonial character would be swept away. Many of these buildings are in that relaxed, languid, flowing idiom that characterises Portuguese Baroque, and it adds an element of human artifice to the beauties of nature.

Outside Paraty small fishing hamlets nestle among the coast's natural forms, and in this stretch is a gated commune (even here, the dangers of Brazil's *favelas* are never far away) of large, single-family houses called

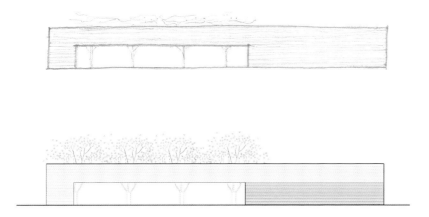

Left: **Du Plessis House, near Paraty, Brazil.**
Sketch *(above)* and elevation *(below),* showing the same idea: a wide and low opening in a stone wall leading to a tree-lined courtyard

Below: **Du Plessis House, near Paraty, Brazil.**
A view into the courtyard: in keeping with
commune rules, the house itself is traditionally
constructed – in this case in Mineira stone

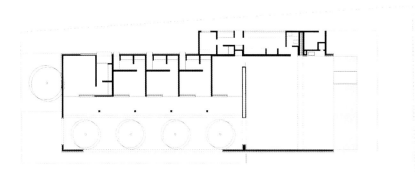

Left: Du Plessis House, near Paraty, Brazil.
Plan: the house essentially consists of a large
living room, four bedrooms and small ancillary
and service areas

Right: **Du Plessis House, near Paraty, Brazil.**
In the courtyard jabuticabeira trees grow from a pebbled ground

Laranjeiras. Within it is the Du Plessis House. Its setting is staggeringly beautiful. A lush, thinly planted plain forms the bottom of a valley between forested hills. Close by are beaches and the sea. It might seem simultaneously inviting, yet so precious that any intervention could be close to sacrilege, and Kogan's response – with a little help from the commune rules – seems to pinpoint this ambiguity.

From the outside it appears to be a large box of Mineira stone from Minas Gerais state, a common Brazilian building material which is laid like slate in thin horizontal strips and rests on rolled steel joists. Though the material is traditional and fairly local, here its form and construction are unashamedly contemporary. Within the box the architecture becomes more conventional, with patios, gently inclined roofs and ceramic tiles. It was, in part, to satisfy the commune's requirement for tiled roofs, but Kogan matches that with his personal inclinations to create a palpable tension between tradition and modernity, yet one which deliberately reverses the standard relationship in locations such as this, where a conventional exterior masks a more contemporary interior.

Kogan finds another level of intensity within this relationship. Openings within the box deliberately contrive views in both directions between inside and outside, implying a connection between the four carefully trained jabuticabeira trees in the pebble-floored courtyard and their more natural and freer counterparts in the landscape – even if that includes a golf course. It is as if the experience of nature had to be rationed and balanced because its full extent would be too much to comprehend. This rationale may bear similarities with those traditions of building in the countryside where human intervention 'corrects' or 'improves' what nature has not quite had the conscious wherewithal to bring to fulfilment, but Kogan's strategy is based on controlling the way of looking, or framing the gaze. It is a theme that Le Corbusier explored and it relies, in the Western tradition at least, on a

Opposite: **Du Plessis House, near Paraty, Brazil.** On two sides of the house the edge of the rainforest comes close

particularly Modernist sensibility; it is the land shorn of individual ownership and economic productivity, served up for aesthetic contemplation. There is much to contemplate.

Given these powerful gestures and the interpretations they offer, the rest of the design is relatively simple and logical. Four bedroom suites open onto a verandah that leads straight to the patio, with its regimented quartet of jabuticabeira trees and the views beyond the stone box. The gridded muxarabi wood screen that divides these rooms from the patio acts as a light filter, so at night the wall seems to emit a luminous glow, and under these conditions the interiors seem to be warm and minimal at the same time. At right angles and looking onto the short side of the patio is a large living room that opens fully onto a terrace on its other side – and a view into the edge of the Atlantic rain forest. In this room stone predominates, as if it were a cavern to provide a protected refuge from which to look into the dense jungle. The windows running the length of the wall fold back completely to make an opening across the full width of the room, but although there is no visual barrier between the urbane and angular room and the forest, the difference in spatial character and the presence of the moat-like swimming pool are more than enough to signify the change.

In a short essay reflecting on a visit he made to the house to photograph it, Kogan contrasts its tranquillity with the chaos of São Paolo, where he has worked since studying architecture there in the 1970s. Arriving back in the city, he writes, was "a shock … [it] is simply appalling". After the rich interplay between untamed nature and human artifice, between the modernity and tradition embodied within the house, almost anywhere might seem shocking.

Right: **Du Plessis House, near Paraty, Brazil.**
Section through the bedroom wing, showing the
essential simplicity of the construction

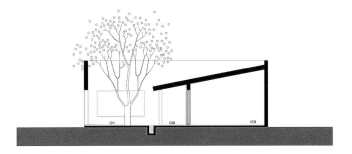

Left: Du Plessis House, near Paraty, Brazil.
A nearly concealed steel beam creates the fiction
of self-supporting 'slates' in the Mineira stone
walls surrounding the courtyard

House Sue

Derick de Bruyn

Irene, Pretoria, South Africa   2002

If South Africa's examples of the country house tradition lived up to its abundance of space and stunning scenery – to say nothing of the opportunities afforded to a privileged minority fully able to spend lavishly – its contribution might rank with the villas of the Veneto, the chateaux of the Loire or the Palladian houses of eighteenth-century British magnates. The truth, needless to say, is more prosaic, but Derick de Bruyn's House Sue indicates how an elegant and seductive form of rural living could emerge from the peculiar possibilities that arise from its position on the cusp between the industrialised and developing worlds, and in relation to its topography on the High Veldt which characterises much of the country. Its slender metal frame and delicately poised roof might give it something in common with the Eames House and its Californian Case Study fellows, while its field stone floor and colouring seem to belong to the soil and culture of Africa. At the very least, this dwelling marks a break with the most familiar idioms of large South African houses, typified by the Cape Dutch style of the early European settlers who spliced Amsterdam gables onto peasant huts, and to which Herbert Baker added a dash of Arts and Crafts in his early twentieth-century homes for the super rich 'Randlords' who had made their fortunes in mining.

But a deeper delving shows this break to be more apparent than real. Such a contrast between industrially produced components and elemental materials is a generic feature of recent architecture elsewhere, though South African conditions give it a seriousness that elevates it to a political act.

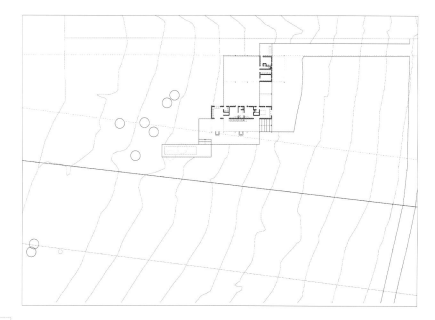

Left: House Sue, Irene, South Africa. Site plan: the site is on a farm in the High Veldt

Opposite: House Sue, Irene, South Africa. "An architectural 'coming to be'", as Derick de Bruyn calls it: simple shelters pregnant with possibilities

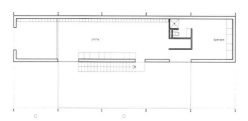

Left: **House Sue, Irene, South Africa.**
First-floor plan: two matching metal frames
define similar spaces for different enclosures
and activities

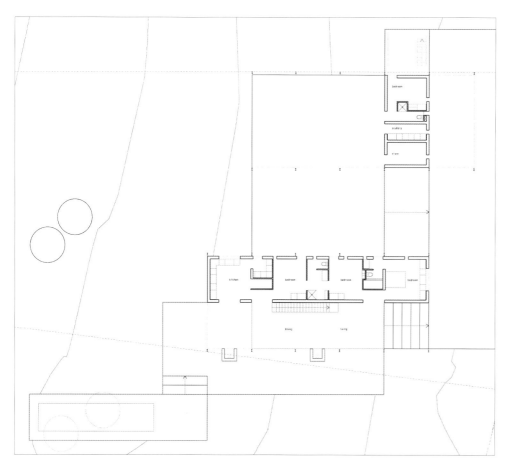

Left: **House Sue, Irene, South Africa.**
Ground-floor plan: private spaces are enclosed,
but the living and dining areas flow freely between
inside and out, on a contiguous floor finish of
field stone paving

Above: **House Sue, Irene, South Africa.** View towards the living area – one fireplace is internal, the other external

Historically its origins run deep; when railways joined the inland gold and diamond fields to the coast in the late nineteenth century, they also opened up the intervening hinterland to manufactured goods from Europe, and many a farmhouse within sight of the tracks acquired the newest and sweetest in factory-made ornament alongside field stone walls. But it also continues through the country's more recent past.

Manifested as the juxtaposition between the most sophisticated technological products and the basic requirements for human shelter – not unlike the satellite dishes to be found in the nearby shanty towns – it is one of the defining characteristics of the country's contemporary condition. The contrast between wealth and poverty is one part of it – but only one part. Related to it is the tension between traditional and progressive belief systems, or between confidence in modern science and dependence on traditional practice. That formidable intellectual load is more than one house can carry, but it does show how the sort of compositional ideas which might, in other locations, be innocent to the point of being almost non-referential, acquire a complexity in the febrile situation of South Africa. Yet it is out of these particular compositional ideas that a new architecture might emerge, if only because addressing them across a broader spectrum is an essential part of dealing with some of the obvious social ills.

House Sue is situated on a farm at Irene on the High Veldt between Johannesburg and Pretoria, where winter nights can be chilly though summers are long, dry and hot. It is on land once owned by J C Smuts, the only South African statesman who achieved international stature – as opposed

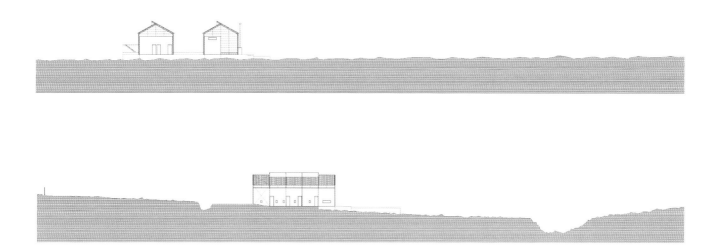

to demonisation – before Nelson Mandela. It is here that he wrote his meditation on the relationship between science and philosophy, *Holism and Evolution* (1926). Though tainted by the predominant beliefs of its time, it did at least look beyond the narrow theocracy of his political rivals.

Having fought the English for this land during the Anglo-Boer War (1899 –1902), Smuts knew well that to make this harsh environment habitable it has to be modified, but he probably would not have foreseen the delicacy that de Bruyn brings to the challenge. House Sue's two similar steel-framed structures owe something to the agricultural sheds common to the area, and in both cases they define a greater volume than is called for by their functions. As if providing a tentatively ordered gradation of public and private space, they are sited parallel to each other, but slightly offset in plan. Within the volume of one there is a solid two-storey box with a small, self-contained residential unit occupying one of its five bays, the rest being entirely open to the elements. Its companion has the bulk of the accommodation. Of its two parts, one is transparent and openable – a contemporary rendition of the traditional *stoep* (verandah) – while the other contains closed and insular spaces. This distinction is partly practical, as the first half naturally becomes a large, open and airy living space which traps winter sun but can be opened for cooling summer draughts, while the enclosed spaces of the second provide scope for retreat and afford varying degrees of protection between the vast landscape and the intimacy of a small interior.

There is also a deeper significance to this distinction. Unlike the clear break between dwelling and context explicit in a formal, European country house or its primitive Cape Dutch cousins, the land here seems to flow from the wild veldt into the private property and under the house, where grass gives way to the field stone floor, as if the manufactured steel frame calls forth

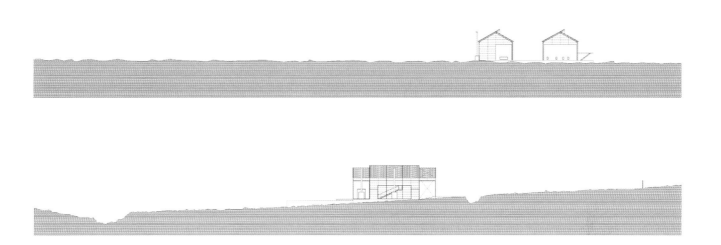

Above: House Sue, Irene, South Africa.
Elevations, from the side *(top)* and looking towards the living room *(above)*. The site slopes gently down towards a shallow riverbed

a different characteristic from the earth itself. From this transparent but covered and protected space, the residents can look out over the land, not as owners or dominators, but as if in symbiotic relationship with it, a relationship that echoes that between the manufactured and raw materials of which the house is built. Each space – whether fully external, covered, enclosed but transparent, or fully enclosed – has a character that is not just a product of the compositional and constructional principles, but assumes its own significance in the relationship between occupants and land.

De Bruyn suggests two points of reference: the simple idea of a tree creating shade and shelter, and the notion of the Greek Chora, or civic space. Such a combination recalls the ideas of his teacher, Barrie Biermann of the University of Natal, who was known to invite guests to meet him for picnics under a tree that would prove to be unique, unmissable and magical in an otherwise treeless landscape, but who also recognised the potential of more sophisticated spatial configurations. Teaching during the high tide of Apartheid, he sought a synthesis between African and Western orderings of space that could be naive or over-subtle to the point of invisibility, but it did at least hold out the hope that some form of interaction was possible. For de Bruyn and others among his students, it provided a seed to nurture in more optimistic times.

That optimism is reflected in House Sue's relationship to the genre of South African farmhouses. This genre is a powerful motif in South African literature – the only cultural activity where it has yet made an international mark. But in comparison with Olive Schreiner's *Story of an African Farm* or J M Coetzee's *Disgrace*, de Bruyn's vision is a sunny one. Perhaps, at some deep level, the political settlement that Smuts could not quite see still lies latent on his old farm.

Right: **House Sue, Irene, South Africa.**
Minimum materials provide maximum volume,
partly for comfort in a harsh climate and partly
because materials are more expensive than
labour

Below: **House Sue, Irene, South Africa.**
Precision-made objects combine with natural
forms and handcraft

Siedlisko Farmhouse

Archistudio
near Krakow, Poland   2003

Coming just shortly after Poland's transition from an authoritarian and centralised regime to a democratic state, Archistudio's Siedlisko farmhouse presented the challenge of rediscovering a way of living, working and building in the countryside that communism had proscribed. Very often, when Poland's nouveaux riches do build, says Malgorzata Pilinkiewicz, who founded Archistudio with Tomasz Studniarek, they want castles or buildings with references to a history that cannot be revived. Pilinkiewicz and Studniarek do know about Polish castles, as they are designing – in a contemporary idiom – three interventions for improving visitor facilities at the historic castle and estate of Lancut in the east of the country. But designing a new house calls for a different approach to aids for interpreting the past, so at Siedlisko they turn for inspiration not to history, but to the landscape itself.

Here, the countryside's forms – powerful almost to the point of being elemental – are deliberately woven into the folds of the site, the upper slope a hill which looks southwards across a broad valley and more distantly to the Tatra Mountains. Retaining walls of local stone follow the contours of the hill and seem to arrest the fall of the land, inscribing a geometrical pattern in it to create a congenial space for habitation. One of the two wings keeps below the line of the hill while the roof of the other starts below the natural ground level but slopes upwards to rise about half a storey above it, the only place where this house of almost 900 square metres uses height to make a statement, and even that is largely concealed from public view by a green roof and a dense tree belt. Such a confident modesty in its size as well as its relationship with the land lends the house a sense of relaxed comfort, and this is the starting point for thinking about its contribution to evolving ideas about lifestyle – and to contemporary Polish architecture.

Above: **Siedlisko Farmhouse, near Krakow, Poland.** The angle between the two wings forms a triangular entrance court

Left: **Siedlisko Farmhouse, near Krakow, Poland.** This computer rendering shows the concept of a house created within volumes formed by retaining walls, engaging with but modifying the landscape

Above: **Siedlisko Farmhouse, near Krakow, Poland.** Though large, the house sits comfortably in the landscape

Understandably, architectural effort in Poland at the moment has to focus on cities. Siedlisko is only a short distance from Krakow, the country's most elegant city where Renaissance palaces line a medieval street pattern, culminating in the magnificent central Marketplace with its great cloth hall. Archistudio is based in the industrial city of Katowice, about 80 kilometres away, and as president of the local chapter of SARP, the Polish society of architects, Studniarek is deeply involved with the regeneration of the town's architectural heritage, almost all of which dates from the twentieth century. But experience of building large apartment blocks – however skilfully massed to conceal their bulk – or austere, concrete, neo-classical cathedrals, or department stores with delicate curtain walls and detailing, is not much use when it comes to designing a contemporary country house.

Precedents in rural architecture are hardly more promising. People did live on and work the land under communism, but at that time the country's leaders were far more interested in using food rationing as an instrument of social policing. Orthodox Marxist theory had far less to say about agriculture than heavy industry, and the drift towards cities that this implied increased pressure on food production without devoting much attention to rural architecture. Where there was new building in the countryside, it aped the grim, prefabricated concrete idiom of the new housing slab blocks that grew up around the expanding cities.

It is against this background that Archistudio's decision to engage with the landscape takes on more significance than a purely functional decision about comfort and privacy. By going into the ground they open up a range of possibilities in spatial and architectural effect. That, in a different way, was Studniarek's and Pilinkiewicz's aim when they established Archistudio in 1992, shortly after completing their studies and gaining some experience in Canada, the UK and the Netherlands. Their early projects were tiny – 20-square-metre shop fit-outs as private enterprise took its first tentative steps towards revival – but, perhaps for this reason, they developed an aptitude for creative effects and clever use of materials. They brought that skill to bear on a slowly expanding portfolio of domestic projects, including their own conversion of a Silesian mineworker's house, but what transformed their prospects was an invitation from a Polish magazine to design a house of the future. Spotted by their client, it led directly to the commission for Siedlisko.

Above: **Siedlisko Farmhouse, near Krakow, Poland.** A gallery leads from the kitchen towards the swimming pool in the second wing

Despite its enviable view, the site is not quite idyllically rural. At the top of the hill are the concrete covers for Krakow's main reservoir, with an untidy collection of buildings around it. But lying behind the house and the newly planted belt of trees around it, they lend some justification to the approach to the house, along a driveway which runs against one of the retaining walls to an acutely angled courtyard, formed between the wall and what seems to be a natural mound that itself runs into a second retaining wall. The long wall is both literally and metaphorically a retaining wall, a stone-edged slice through the hill which makes the frame for excavating a garage, staff flat and swimming pool behind and below the slope of the hill – in reality a green roof.

As the drive descends, the topography of the site leads naturally to the second wing of the house, its wood cladding contrasting with the long stone retaining wall. An equally natural material, the wood's warmth and less forbidding character make it an appropriate material for the entrance to the house's main accommodation. If there are architectural precedents, they

Right and below: **Siedlisko Farmhouse, near Krakow, Poland.** Three elevations: the west elevation of the main house, with its adjacent retaining wall *(right)*; the long elevation of the swimming pool wing facing onto the entrance court *(below)*; and the south elevation of the main house wing *(bottom)*

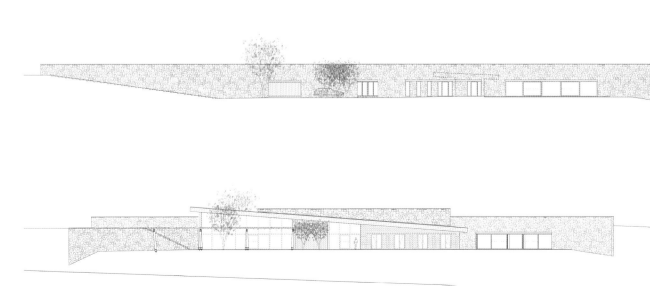

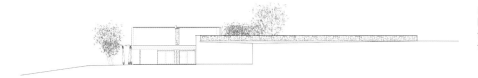

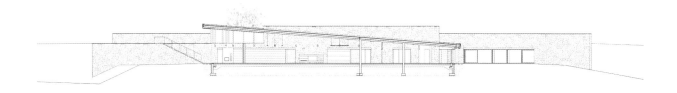

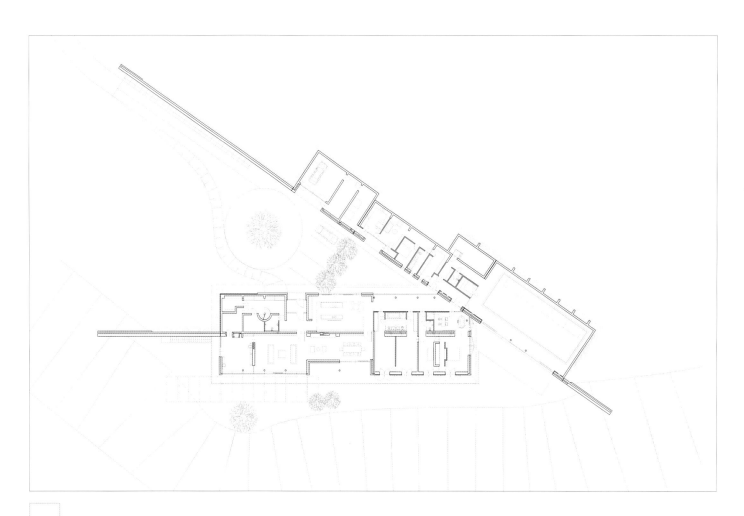

Above: **Siedlisko Farmhouse, near Krakow, Poland.** A belt of trees has been planted around the house

come more from the American tradition of Frank Lloyd Wright and Marcel Breuer, both of whom knew a thing or two about field stone, elemental forms and large volumes, but these are remote influences.

The house's planning is quite simple. Splitting the accommodation into two blocks makes a logical functional distinction, and allowing the ancillary wing to slide beyond the main one means the swimming pool has a window to the view. The principal wing contains an entrance, kitchen, generous bedrooms, and a large living room whose ceiling slopes upwards from the dining end, through the sitting area to a separate study, echoing the gradient of the drive. Each of these spaces and the bedrooms front a terrace with a banked lawn sloping down to an artificial pool, before the landscape regains its original form. Inside the effects come from volume, light and texture. Concrete columns offset rough and smooth stone finishes on the walls, while floors are largely wooden with polished stone in the entrance.

When the client – a publisher who needed shelves for 5000 books – bought the site of about 40 hectares, he found it had once formed part of an aristocratic estate. Taking advantage of a law which allows the building of new homes in the countryside for people actively engaged in farming – this is still a working farm, though not the owner's principal source of income – he was able to commission a house that demonstrates a more relaxed way of living than the more regulated, hierarchical precedent afforded by the country houses of the old aristocracy, as well as being freer and more leisured than anything the communists would have countenanced.

Opposite: **Siedlisko Farmhouse, near Krakow, Poland.** Though its form is derived closely from the site, the plan has many of the characteristics of new country houses: a grand entrance, large living and entertaining spaces, a generous kitchen, indoor swimming pool and staff accommodation – here between the pool and garage

NARRATIVE

Group of Family Houses

Leroy Street Studio

Long Island, New York, USA 2002 – 2006 *(ongoing project)*

At the end of *The Great Gatsby*, F Scott Fitzgerald has his narrator imagine how the landscape of Long Island induced a "capacity for wonder" in the first Europeans to see it. He referred to a time before Thomas Jefferson's decision to impose a grid across the vast and wondrous expanses of North America, subjecting the land to the orderings of the human and, in Jefferson's case, capitalist mind. Now it is no longer the natural scenery of Long Island that would encourage visitors to wonder, but the way humans have made this sliver of land their plaything. As a retreat from the city, this group of three houses for members of the same family (the third is designed but not yet built) may typify this change of emphasis, but the way the design develops and

Left: **Family Houses, Long Island, USA.** The site plan, showing the semi-ordered insertion of landscape features and walls that informs the layout of the buildings. The main house is tucked into the south-west corner, with the daughter's house beside it, a little to the east

Above: **Family Houses, Long Island, USA.** The late afternoon sun illuminates the bedroom of the daughter's house in the foreground, as well as the parents' house beyond

interweaves various themes also makes it a knowing reflection on the experience of modernity – of which the process of subjugating the American landscape was a part.

Another part of the move away from nature was the rapid growth of cities like New York, which generated both the need and the economic wherewithal for retreat, and these houses imply that it still does. From the dense perimeter planting to the intimate and contained spaces of the interiors, the design supports its primary purpose of refuge. But in doing so it adopts some elemental principles of Modernist composition, and this strategy places the design within a recognisable architectural genre.

Flat and lightly treed, the site is strangely receptive to a Modernist aesthetic, and the austerely elegant site plan starts to make these relationships explicit. It clearly shows the perimeter planting and how the shape derives from the ubiquitous North American grid. Although only a couple of blocks from the ocean from where Fitzgerald's Dutch sailors may have landed, this is a landscape marked with human intervention. Within the precinct defined by the perimeter planting is a series of far more delicate figures. These are straight but rough stone walls, sometimes meeting, sometimes gliding past

each other. Running parallel to the site boundaries, there are just enough of them to introduce an orthogonal grid onto the site, but not enough to inscribe it absolutely. Instead there is an interplay between order and randomness, a common Modernist motif, but also an analogy with family relationships.

The site plan has a faint echo of those early Mondrian paintings where trees assume an abstract form, and a rather stronger one of Mies van der Rohe's early brick houses, where apparently rational compositions are shot through with enigmatic qualities. As with Mies, at points the walls seem to coalesce to define spaces with greater specificity and, as they do so, they are joined by running water, first a tiny rill and then a larger flume which discharges into the swimming pool. These conjunctions create the conditions in which the houses are organised, and they occur as if by the inexorable logic of Modernist composition.

The main house, for the parents, stands slightly apart from the other two – one built for the daughter and the other proposed for the son – which are arranged around a common court with their compositions more closely interlocked. As they define the houses, the walls' dual purposes manifest themselves, transforming from loose and abstract indicator of randomness and order to a more specific and physical role of protecting internal spaces and showing where they might be entered. Both by their thickness and texture, and by sheltering outdoor spaces, the walls introduce a series of layers between exterior and interior.

Left: Family Houses, Long Island, USA.
Looking across the dining area into the living room of the main house, with its expansive views of the garden beyond

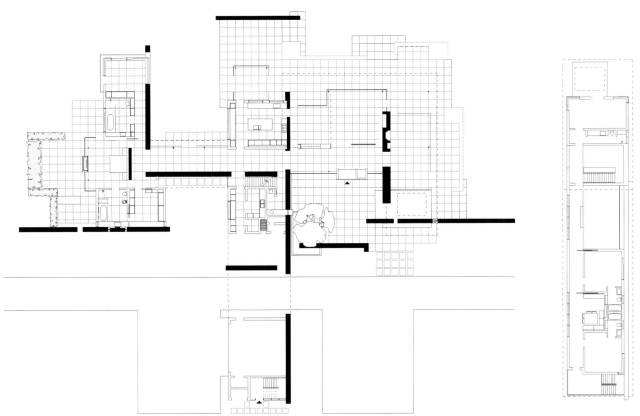

Understandably, the parents' house is the largest and reached first from the edge of the site. Approached from the south, it appears quite solid and the few gaps in the walls give the merest glimpse into the world beyond. A driveway leads under a bridge so its entrance is concealed until the walls part and stone paving projects beyond them to invite visitors into an open court with a beautiful Japanese maple tree: one side of this court is glazed onto the entrance hall. Here new vistas open and experiences take shape. Wall and ceiling planes define a complex volume, leaving gaps between them for views to the outside and for light to penetrate. Straight ahead, the largely glazed wall opens onto the private gardens, where expansively volumetric trees and the stone walls might inspire thoughts about composition or nature, or merely serve to offer the relaxing qualities of an enclosed and calm precinct. There is much of Frank Lloyd Wright and more than a touch of Marcel Breuer's larger houses, but the spaces seem less crabbed than the former's could be, and less didactically heavy than the latter's.

This house has an essentially cruciform plan. One axis runs between the public spaces of hall, dining and sitting rooms and covered porch, via a gallery to the principal bedroom suite. The cross axis, marked by the bridge, has ancillary spaces: garages and kitchen on the ground floor, staff and guest accommodation above. However, that simple diagram belies the care taken to ensure each main space has its own crafted and contrived relationship with its own constituent parts, and the outside.

Beyond the main house are those of the children, and their smaller scale allows them to be less formal and more freely composed, though the basic concepts are closely related. In the daughter's house massive walls again act as barriers but leave small, protected, interstitial spaces between themselves and the actual limits of the building. The contrasting architectural expression of the two arms of its L-shaped plan reflects their functions. The bedroom wing, enclosed in Glu-lam portal frames and timber louvres, is contained, while the other wing – comprising kitchen, dining and sitting rooms – seems to extend by continuation of its walls outwards and engage with the landscape.

Given that these houses are retreats for affluent urbanites they need no programme or meaning beyond relaxation, comfort and privacy. That even the most basic nuclear family of parents, a son and a daughter has almost endless relational permutations hardly needs to be spelt out. But with its knowing references to Modernist composition and that genre of houses made respectable by Wright and Breuer, it shows how a Modernist approach to design in the landscape can create the tranquillity the programme demands.

Below: **Family Houses, Long Island, USA.**
View of the parents' house from the garden, with
the main living areas to the left and the master
bedroom suite, clad in wood, to the far right, with
a glazed corridor connecting them

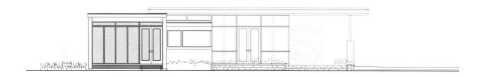

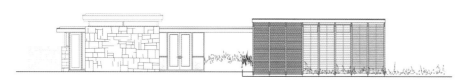

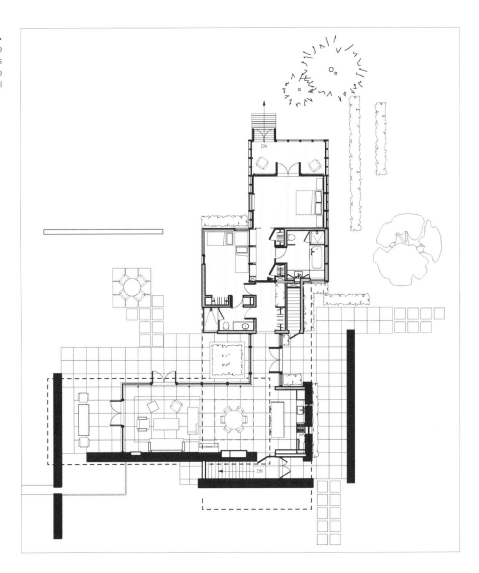

Right: **Family Houses, Long Island, USA.**
The L-shaped plan of the daughter's house, the
bedroom wing separated from the living areas
by a short glazed corridor that also forms the
entrance hall

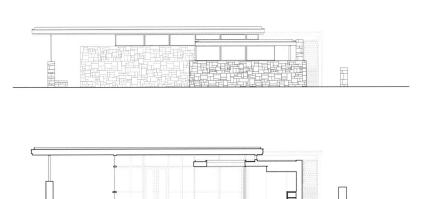

Above: **Family Houses, Long Island, USA.** The
south elevation of the daughter's house and a
matching section through the main living areas

Left: **Family Houses, Long Island, USA.** A view
of the living room of the daughter's house, with
its extended roof providing shade and weather
protection to a small external sitting area

New Hill

John Winter

Hampshire, Southern England, UK 2003

As an unashamedly Modernist country house built in the English countryside in the twenty-first century, New Hill is a rare phenomenon indeed. It is remarkable in not dissembling its modernity by disguising itself within the shell of a barn or the precinct of an existing building. Its flat roof, steel structure and grey brick walls are exposed for all to see, or so it would seem. Predictably the planning authority stipulated that a modern design would only be acceptable if it were not visible from the road, and was only prepared to

Below: **New Hill, Hampshire, UK.** Modernism returns to the English countryside as a series of single-storey pavilions, each accommodating a different function

countenance Modernism at all because the site was previously used as a breaker's yard. On a fine balance English planners might concede that a Modernist design is less of an eyesore than dismembered and rusting vehicles. It would seem that no-one made the wryly ironic suggestion that they were merely swapping what might, to some, look like a display of contemporary art for modern architecture.

John Winter, New Hill's architect, brought to the brief and site a sophisticated and acute understanding of Modernism which allowed him to exploit this rare opportunity to the full. In true Modernist fashion he pays close attention to the possibilities of the site and the functional programme. Given the planning demand for invisibility, the house could only have two storeys if the lower floor was tucked into the slope, which rises from the road towards the south. The best views, meanwhile, are looking north and can only be obtained from the upper floor. These two conditions naturally suggested putting the main accommodation above the ancillary spaces. Placing the main bedroom suite on the same level was also logical, and the clients' requirement for it to have an easterly aspect led Winter to express it as a separate volume. Combining these various factors resulted in the overall concept of the house as a series of steel-and-glass pavilions linked by grey brick walls, all resting on a solid podium.

Such a logical response to empirical conditions is certainly a Modernist approach, but Winter is steeped in Modernism's culture as well as its pragmatics. The architectural historian and critic Reyner Banham, a family friend, encouraged his interest in architecture even before he went to the Architectural Association in the early 1950s. A few years earlier Modernism had been adopted as the architectural idiom of the new Welfare State in Britain, and quite what form it should take was hotly debated at the AA and in the pages of Banham's employer, *The Architectural Review*. On graduating Winter won a scholarship to Yale, pioneering a path that Norman Foster and Richard Rogers would follow a few years later. While in the US he also absorbed ideas about form and composition from Josef Albers, who was

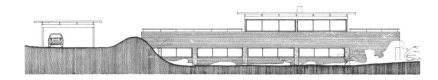

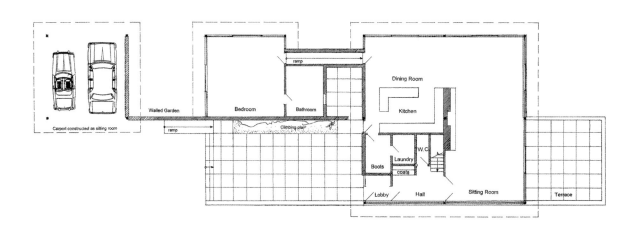

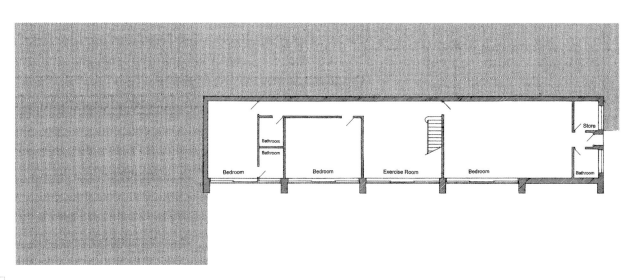

head of Fine Arts at Yale. Arguably most important of all was a trip he made across the US to pay homage to the Eames House in Pacific Palisades. He marvelled at the lightness of material and fineness of detail of this and other Case Study Houses. After he returned to the UK he worked for Ernö Goldfinger, whose designs tended to be more massive. Winter has played on this contrast throughout his career.

New Hill certainly shows traces of this influence. The crisply and elegantly detailed flat roof rests on rolled steel joists that cantilever beyond the walls of the house, allowing their construction to be clearly visible from the exterior, but also performing the practical task of shading the glass walls from the sun. Square on plan, the main pavilion appears to be simplicity itself. It shares the Case Study ideals of generous light and freely flowing space that seem to increase their size, a sense reinforced by the elegant and legible structure. As it was treated as a single-storey building the steel needed no fire protection, and there are no fussy joints or details where the steel members meet, just an elegant fusion. In turn they rest on a ring beam, itself supported on corner and one intermediate column on each wall, which creates a little clerestory gap between the top of the ring beam and underside of the roof. A central wall establishes a line which divides the sitting room from all other areas. Yet the corner entrance and the route through a lobby and hall into the sitting room seem to imply a circulation pattern that follows the perimeter, which would lead from the entrance through the sitting room to culminate in the dining room. Winter spent long enough in Albers' aura to realise that the square is anything but a neutral form. Concealed from this route are the boot room and laundry, and the kitchen only becomes visible from the dining room. Notionally the route continues down a ramp to the second pavilion, with the main bedroom which also enjoys southerly views.

If there are clear Californian influences, Winter also draws on other aspects of the diverse Modernist tradition. The brick walls wend their way

around the house, and though ceding to the pavilions where they meet, do add another spatial dimension. On the east side of the main bedroom and part of the sitting room's glazed west facade, they enclose small outside courtyards in a manner that recalls Mies van der Rohe's seductive, single-storey courtyard houses of the 1920s, which explored the tension between transparent and solid definitions of space. And in the use of brick and fenestration on the lower level, there could be a hint of 1930s English Modernism, a phase of architectural history with which Winter is very familiar, and to which he has contributed much with skilful restorations of several of its more notable examples.

In this aspect of his work Winter has become aware of the deficiencies in thermal performance of early Modernist buildings and has done much to devise ways of bringing them up to contemporary environmental standards. At first glance New Hill might seem liable to repeat some of the earlier mistakes. But the high energy performance of the earthbound lower level together with immensely careful detailing of the steel frame to minimise cold bridging brings it up overall to contemporary requirements.

Modernism and the English country house never fully consummated the mild flirtation they enjoyed in the 1930s in such examples as High and Over by Amyas Connell and Basil Ward (1930), or Serge Chermayeff's Bentley Wood (1938). But at New Hill, after 70 years in which both traditions have had to question their very existence, Winter shows how they might come together to meet the very different circumstances of today.

Right: **New Hill House, Hampshire, UK.** A view of the dining area through to the internal kitchen

Left: **New Hill, Hampshire, UK.** The clear construction and a controlled palette of finishes and materials invite a Modernist lifestyle

Old Wardour House

Eric Parry Architects

Wiltshire, Southern England, UK   2003

All around Old Wardour House lie traces of history that reach out and reverberate across the landscape. Surrounded by a hunting forest since Saxon times, site of Old Wardour Castle since the late fourteenth century and of New Wardour Castle since the 1770s – when the surrounding park was also redesigned – the whole area, and not just the individual buildings within it, seems to have the story of aristocratic rural living inscribed into it. Through its relationship with this landscape, Eric Parry's extension to Old Wardour House gains its significance. As well as giving the house a new focus that reorients it towards the needs of contemporary life, the extension interweaves those needs with strands of the site's historic narrative so that both can co-exist into the future.

In comparison to the splendidly picturesque backdrop provided by the ruinous Old Wardour Castle and the brooding austerity of the Neo-Palladian new castle about one mile distant, Old Wardour House is modest and unassuming. The scale of the extension could not in itself compete with either, so only a subtle strategy could relate it to its neighbours. What has emerged is not just a skilful design that caters to modern domestic requirements, but also a gently thought-provoking commentary on what it might mean to live in such a charged landscape, and so offer a small contribution to a possible future for the English country house tradition.

Below: **Old Wardour House, Wiltshire, UK.** Built for a younger son, Old Wardour House soon became the estate manager's residence

Left: **Old Wardour House, Wiltshire, UK.** Site plan: redolent with six hundred years of country house history, Old Wardour House sits alongside one of the outer walls of the magnificent late fourteenth-century Old Wardour Castle

The version of English aristocratic life narrated at Wardour flits around the typical stories of the ebb and flow in fortunes of land-owning families in general, and the themes peculiar to the family who owned the house from the 1560s: the Arundells. Built by the Lovell family in the fourteenth century, Old Wardour Castle dates from a time when castles were already becoming outdated, when leisure and an evocation of a mythologised and idealised history had superseded defence as their *raison d'être*. During the sixteenth century, Robert Smythson – architect of nearby Longleat and one of the originators of the country house tradition – 'modernised' it, adding a few Serlian touches. Only in the following century did it undergo a real siege – in 1643, during the English Civil War – when gunpowder proved what architects and their clients already knew: that castles were romantic anachronisms. Ironically, the person who blew it up was its Royalist owner, the second Lord Arundell, who wanted to flush out the occupying Parliamentary forces. If that were not peculiar in itself, the Arundell family remained Roman Catholic and so could not fully enjoy the privileges wealth and rank might have brought them, at least until the 1770s when a glimmer of religious emancipation allowed them to commission James Paine to

Left: **Old Wardour House, Wiltshire, UK.** Part elevation: Parry deliberately used the same stone on the extension as that of the main house, but treats it differently, with deep, chamfered windows

design the new castle about a mile distant *(see page 9)*. In a second ruination, the old castle was reshaped into a picturesque folly.

Though Old Wardour House itself only dates from the early nineteenth century, traces of this recusant history are all around. Alongside its foundations runs a tunnel large enough for a man to pass through, while one of its seventeenth-century outbuildings has exquisite classical details. Both imply that Jesuit priests were present; it is known that they took refuge with and gave spiritual comfort to the Arundells. The tunnel afforded means of escape, while the details might have marked their chapel.

The original house is essentially a simple rectilinear structure under a pitched roof dating from the early nineteenth century, with an adjoining barn that is probably a little older. Originally built for a younger Arundell son, it soon became the estate manager's residence. In the early 1960s the present owners' mother and stepfather bought the house when it was in poor condition, and their restoration included converting the barn into a luscious library, with the rest conforming to the conventions of the time: a drawing room, a formal dining room, a kitchen facing north onto the service yard and a nursery somewhat detached from the rest of the house.

Following the logic of its construction, the house has a central spine running along its length, dividing the original accommodation into two ranges. That axis terminates in the extension. Containing the only rooms which span the full width of the house, the extension opens a whole range of spatial and formal opportunities for Parry to exploit. Gone are the once rigid barriers

Above: **Old Wardour House, Wiltshire, UK.** Part elevation: the remnants of an existing wall conceal a first-floor terrace

Opposite: **Old Wardour House, Wiltshire, UK.** Ground-floor plan: the wing on the left is the library, converted some time ago from a barn, while the small cottage on the other side of the entrance court is elaborately ornamented, possibly because it was once used as a Jesuit chapel

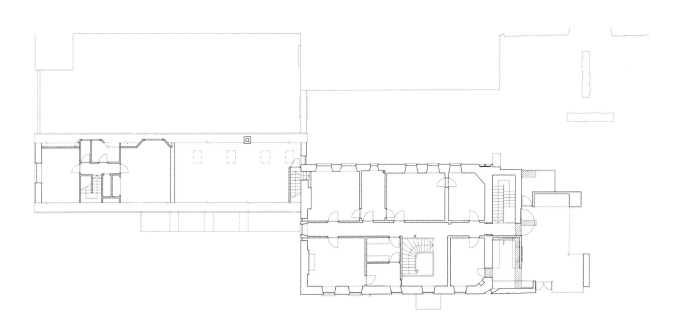

Below: **Old Wardour House, Wiltshire, UK.**
First-floor plan: the new extension is on the right
end of the main house, with hatching denoting
those walls that were demolished

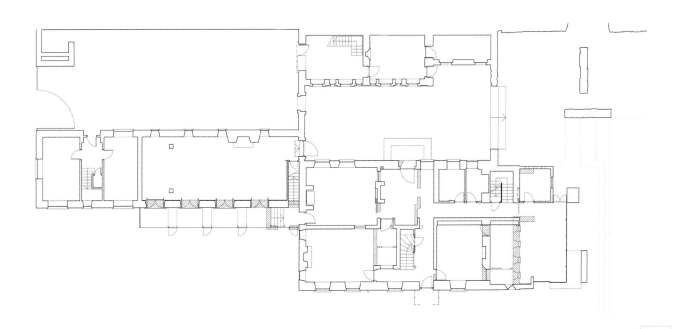

between cooking and eating, 'withdrawing' and dining, inside and outside. Instead of these activities being delineated by axially aligned rooms with orthogonally organised walls, they can now intermingle in the dining kitchen which occupies most of the extension's ground floor, and whose limits and relationships, notably to the garden, are far less clear than in the original rooms. Glass walls seem to prevent the inside space reaching a stone pier, but slide open to allow access to the terrace and lawn beyond, implying that life now is perhaps freer, richer and maybe offers more opportunity. Above is a principal bedroom suite that has a level of comfort and generosity of space, light and views that capture something of the complex interaction which characterises a successful marriage. As well as the obvious provisions of bathroom and dressing room, there are protected niches and secret vistas, again shaped by the carefully placed glass walls and stone piers that form connections both to the landscape and to emotions which may be private or shared. It allows a subtle commentary on the way owners of a country house might engage in a reciprocal relationship with their surroundings.

Parry's use of stone demonstrates how he weaves a skein of connections between past and present, both in tangible and ethereal terms. Quarried and used extensively locally, the stone itself joins geological with historical time, as the way it has been used and the marks that individual pieces bear are themselves testimony to an interaction between humans and nature. Textured or smooth, it glows in sunlight, but acquires an austere, greyish hue when in shadow, giving it an intense physical presence. In some elements, such as incorporating an angled buttress into the new wall, Parry plays on these tactile qualities. Part of the new wall uses stones which may well have come from the castle, so the texture is consistent across old and new though the line of the buttress is clearly visible. Where new stonework is detached from the old, it is smooth and refined – as if imitating the characteristic of the glass that creates the separation – and inviting the striations of a future experience that will themselves become history. If the physicality of the stone can indicate a future, the implication runs, then the whole complex bundle of emotions, values and ambitions that are tied up in the house and its owners could have one too.

Right: **Old Wardour House, Wiltshire, UK.**
The house sits in a small hanging valley, ringed by
dense woodland. The area has been devoted to
rural leisure since Saxon times, when it was a
hunting park

Left: Old Wardour House, Wiltshire, UK. The tiny extension continues the gradual evolution of the park through building and other interventions, making it a palimpsest of country living

Sphinx Hill

John Outram

Oxfordshire, Southern England, UK   2000

Among the sodality of great rivers, the Thames does not have quite the same status as the Nile. Its source was rather easier to track; it could be laid end to end about 20 times along the other's length, and though its role in English culture is undeniable, it was hardly responsible for nurturing one of the world's first civilisations. Yet whether mighty waterway or a tiny stream, argues John Outram, all rivers evoke the primal moment when time began to flow. Appreciating the particular character of an individual river affords an opportunity to contemplate that event, and so to muse on culture in general. Weaving a narrative through his sophisticated grasp of architectural iconography, Outram's design for Sphinx Hill explores this intriguing territory between reality and myth, and inscribes it in a quintessentially English setting on the bank of the River Thames.

This exploration begins in the simple juxtaposition of name and site. The word 'sphinx' immediately evokes Ancient Egypt and there are statues of those inscrutable creatures in the garden. The real presence of the Thames at the bottom of the garden makes the notion of a river inescapable: by coming together, river and Egypt evoke the Nile, the guarantor of Ancient Egyptian civilisation. This reference is not arbitrary, as the clients are expert in and enthusiastic about that culture, and it is also one of the sources for Outram's personal iconography. But neither party wanted a slavishly archaeological recreation of Ancient Egyptian architecture. Instead, mindful that domestic buildings were not its high point, each was interested in the possibilities Egyptian iconography might have for contemporary life. So even before design work started, a layer of mythical possibility infused the typically

Above: **Sphinx Hill, Oxfordshire, UK.** A page from Outram's copious sketchbooks: curves and grids suggest flow and stasis

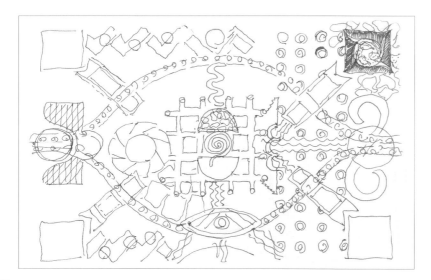

Left: **Sphinx Hill, Oxfordshire, UK.** The 'eternal forest' of columns on a regular grid acquires a specificity when a river flows through it, bringing the concept of diachronic time

Opposite: **Sphinx Hill, Oxfordshire, UK.** The house itself: an 'eternal forest' through which flows a 'river' (just out of picture to the right) that eventually reaches the 'ocean' (the River Thames, at the bottom of the garden). A 'flying raft' has alighted on some of the trees in the forest, turning them into columns for a house

SPANDREL/
FLOOR EDGE.

BIG "COSMIC"
MEANING

DOMESTIC
MEANING

Typical moulding along the
edge of a floor meaning
that the floor is "born"
from the sea.

The upper floors are
also "grounded".

an Egyptian boat, like
the one that carries the
sun

Also the boat of the
"Colonists" that carries the
"hearth fire".

wings carrying the sun.

The hearth fire can also be
"flown" - magic carpet

wings in the shape of
a boat.

another way of showing that
the hearth fire can
either sail or fly.

"upper" fire

raft-cum-house-shrine

boat-cum-wings supporting the "house"
inner fire

ICONOGRAPHY
OF THE
HOUSE
WINDOW &
SPANDREL

Left: **Sphinx Hill, Oxfordshire, UK.** Outram
relates "big cosmic meanings" to everyday
experience

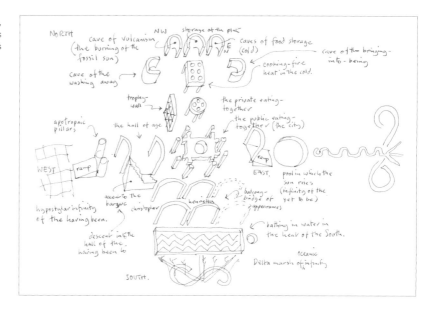

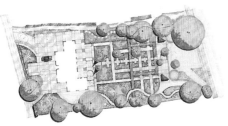

Above: **Sphinx Hill, Oxfordshire, UK.** Site plan, showing the inscribed grid extending around the house and into the garden, through which water flows on its way to the River Thames

Opposite: **Sphinx Hill, Oxfordshire, UK.** The house is rich in meaning and commanding in presence

English pastoral setting. The completed house makes it explicit, interweaving mythical references and cultural ideas with practical needs and human comforts to forge a connection between the cerebral and the sensory.

Outram uses the whole site as well as features beyond it to develop his narrative. A regular tartan grid is expressed in the forecourt and the terrace as well as the house itself. For Outram this is "the forest of the eternal present", a concept he finds in Serlio's first building, the Meeting House of Athens, where 500 columns stake out a regular grid, except that Outram's columns are sometimes sublimated into squares on the ground. There is no variety and so time stands still. But as soon as water starts to flow, so does time and so the river valley becomes the counterpoint to the forest. Outram gives the house two 'valleys' – or cross axes – around which it is composed.

Its forms, colours and ornament are exuberant and arresting, but that effect is underwritten and enhanced by a gradually dawning sense of order and discipline. It is, after all, essentially symmetrical. The principal volumes rise to a second storey above a wider single-level base and are clearly expressed with three shallow barrel vaults, the central one being higher and slightly recessed to emphasise the primary axis, which runs from the entrance through the house and beyond into the garden.

Expressed as pure volumes this composition could almost be Modernist, but for Outram volume and form alone are not sufficient. He uses colour and ornament, both to reinforce the volumetric effect and then to add extra nuances and interpretations. The buff colour, for instance, implies stone, and used in vertical panels it moves easily into a suggestion of columns. So much is logical, as all buildings need support, but in an imaginative leap the red circle within the V-shaped 'capital' goes further, defining the end of the arched beams while also symbolically showing the sun rising above mountains and acting as a hieroglyph for a boat. The sky blue fascia reinforces the literal interpretation, while the entablature and roof above subvert logic to enter the realm of imagination and myth. For Outram, the roof is a mythical raft which floats in the heavens before alighting at particular points on Earth – an interpretation inferred in the word 'rafter', so it is no accident that the rafters

here are given visual accentuation and the roof eaves are turned upwards, as if the prow and stern of a boat. An iconography that started in logic and reason transforms, as it travels upwards, into a flight of fantasy.

Outram remarks about the beam/sun/boat motif that he enjoys showing how a primitive building method can refer to the exotic, and reveals that he is as keen as any Modernist on exploiting the expressive possibilities of construction. The difference is that his work also references non-architectural ideas, using buildings as vehicles for conveying meaning beyond themselves. Similarly, the internal planning starts with an appreciation of physical needs and uses them as a springboard to evoke other references. The symmetrical entrance front fixes the front door, and establishes an axis through the dining room to the garden, where its status as a mythical valley is made explicit by becoming a stream of water which leads to the Thames – in this relationship standing for the ocean. The vista looking east from the dining room takes the eye over a formal garden, which might recall a God's eye view of the Nile Valley with ordered fields and orthogonal irrigation channels. On either side regular civilisation breaks down into free-flowing lines and ultimately a forest of trees. A secondary axis/valley crosses the first in the dining room, marking its importance as space, and making the appropriate if slyly humorous connection between larder and swimming pool at either end of the axis. Comfort, function and myth seem to merge, and the rich colour schemes reinforce the union of the sensory and the symbolic.

Living in the house is more than a wonderful and intellectually challenging fantasy; it is practically adapted to everyday life. The central entrance leads to a dining room, with a generous kitchen on one side and with studies and the pool on the other. A cleverly turned stair leads from the entrance, over the door, to a magnificent, barrel-vaulted first-floor sitting room, complete with pyramidal fireplace and an oculus that plays sunlight on the underside of the ceiling, as if it were the moon in the heavens. Bedrooms flank this space.

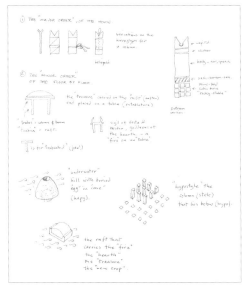

Above: **Sphinx Hill, Oxfordshire, UK.** By evoking age-old cultural symbols, Outram shows how architecture can relate to broader intellectual ideas

Outram's narrative unfolds through many subtle twists. It depends on an appreciation of the relationship between form and function, but one that is more multilayered than a functionalist could ever allow. It uses colour, ornament, image, texture, form and space to build up a kaleidoscope of impression and experience by literal reference, hint and analogy. It exudes generosity, both in terms of hospitality and also – though perhaps more difficult to convey – intellectual generosity, through its clever and appropriate use of narrative to convey meaning. Here ideas mingle with comfort, and evocations of fantasy and archaeology with today's practical needs, perhaps the finest combination a domestic building can have.

Below: **Sphinx Hill, Oxfordshire, UK.** Culture eventually yields to nature – the formal garden giving way to more natural planting to either side and untouched water meadow and woodland on the far side of the River Thames

Lower Mill Estate

Richard Reid Architects and others
Cirencester, Gloucestershire, UK   2005

Of all the reasons for building a house in the country, the strongest and most common motivation behind the houses that feature in this book is the urge to satisfy varying concepts of leisure with different depths of pocket. Given that leisure is so powerful a force in contemporary society, and bearing in mind the long history of retreating to the countryside for relaxation, that is hardly surprising. Lower Mill Estate – where a series of landmark houses by architects such as Will Alsop and Piers Gough will arise amid the surprisingly Arcadian landscape of former gravel pits – echoes the age-old idea of rustic retreats, but resounds also with the aesthetic and economic consequences of a society where leisure is not just available to the privileged few, but has become one of the largest industries in the developed world.

The site comprises 550 acres of largely flat landscape outside Cirencester very close to the Cotswold Hills, a beautiful area of rolling scenery and elegant stone buildings set among lavish gardens, where affluent Londoners have been buying second homes for so long that locals cannot stay and only the wealthy can penetrate. Jeremy Paxton, a helicopter-owning property developer spotted the former gravel pits, which in British planning parlance are designated 'brownfield' and so far easier to redevelop than pristine green fields, and started to plan a leisure village. After several iterations which involved building relatively small, neo-vernacular units, he decided to up the stakes and build up to 46 'landmark' houses, stretching the conventions of English taste in rural living to the extreme. The first eight designs were launched in the summer of 2005.

Purchasers of these houses need not fret about the moral state of their tenantry and of broader society, as any self-respecting Victorian country house builder did; nor are they likely to be seeking preferment from capricious, miserly and itinerant monarchs who might be gratified by a display of lavish hospitality, as the builders of the Elizabethan prodigy houses sought. They are not likely, either, to see these houses as settings where their art collections might allow their names and taste, if not their souls, to achieve immortality. But, above all, they are not experimenting with and creating their own taste, a pastime that fascinated country house builders like Lord Burlington and Giangiorgio Trissino, whose circle included many of Palladio's early patrons. Instead, they will buy a house that is already designed and branded, even if it has scope for modification.

The responsibility for making such a house falls largely to the masterplanning architect, Richard Reid. He has matured his own approach to domestic design over several decades, largely in affluent suburbs where he

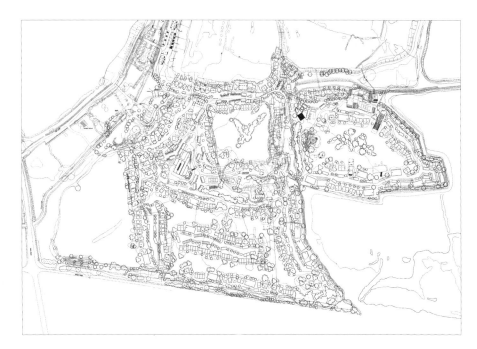

Left: **Lower Mill Estate, Gloucestershire, UK.**
Richard Reid Architects' proposed site layout

has found scope for innovative domestic design, weaving in his predilections for the Californian Case Study Houses with inventive interpretations of the suburban vernacular. Though Lower Mill is not his first venture into country houses, it is certainly his most extensive. Without the suburban surroundings to temper his imagination, his own house here shows the Californian influence. It is a disk that cantilevers from a central core and seems to hover over the reed bank at the water's edge. It rotates and its photovoltaic cell-covered roof panels open to maximise comfort and energy efficiency, while the necessarily fluid space planning of such a form takes its occupants about as far from the rigid social hierarchies of traditional country houses as is feasible. But whoever buys this house is likely to be more attracted to the subterranean screening room than by the hunting and shooting or the political power that once came from a Parliamentary Rotten Borough.

Other designs cater for different tastes. Piers Gough's house may lack its own cinema, but within its irregular, ascending helical form – rising from the water itself – are a wet boathouse and, on top, a swimming pool. In between are four bedrooms and a large living room. Alison Brooks is more cerebral, evoking the artist James Turrell as well as earlier single-storey Modernist houses in an austere composition of planes and forms, where light and texture provide the ornament. Standing on its own island, Will Alsop's house encloses a large volume, of which nearly half is given over to a winter garden which, though open at one end, might bring a dash of the subtropics to the Cotswolds. Amorphous forms containing bedrooms hang within the volume, while the living areas, a dining table, sofa, armchair and grand piano are on a plate that can slide from the enclosed part of the volume into the winter garden or even beyond, to hover like a giant diving board over the lake. Capability Brown never contrived anything quite like that. Sutherland Hussey Architects' timber louvre box will appeal to those who want to live in orthogonal regularity, while those who want the comfort of curves might feel drawn to Sarah Featherstone's Orchid House, where each activity seems to

Opposite: **Lower Mill Estate, Gloucestershire, UK.** The original landmark house, Somerford Villa, designed by Richard Reid. Its success convinced Jeremy Paxton and Reid that they should curate a series of more radical designs in key locations across the estate

have its own petal-like form to define it. Eva Jiricna and the Californian Roger Sherman complete the roster of architects for the first eight, and as clients buy them prior to construction – for up to £5.5 million – they will be able to influence the detailed design.

The landmark houses at Lower Mill are inherently paradoxical, being both within a tradition of country houses and, in some ways, antithetical to it. The question is whether these antitheses to country house conventions are part of the evolution of that tradition for the twenty-first century, or the contradictions that prove it to be, finally, dead. Though these houses offer opportunities for rural leisure activities, albeit with a stronger bias to the aquatic than the traditional equine, the relationships they engender with site and social context mark a strong break with the general understanding of what hitherto constituted country house conventions. Potential owners – who may have several homes and spend no more than a few weeks in each – may be delighted that the estate company will assume responsibility for maintaining the grounds, but they will hardly have the sense of ownership and rootedness that comes with such responsibility. And though there will be an implied hierarchy between the owners of the lavish landmark houses and their less affluent neighbours, it will not carry the obligation to enforce social order as lords of the manor were obliged to do.

Lower Mill splits open the country house tradition. It abolishes the sense of being connected within a complex social web and particular physical environment that is almost inevitable in a conventional country house. Where the significance of a country house once depended on a balance of social contact and aesthetic experience, these ones, their social contact commuted to a hefty management charge, will depend almost entirely on design. The ability to pay a purchase price that might buy a small estate is part of an ineluctable process of globalisation, which itself brings new forms of social and economic relations. It is within them that new country houses will be conceived and built; Lower Mill gives an indication of what form they might take.

Above: **Lower Mill Estate, Gloucestershire, UK.** An alternative view of Sundance Villa by Richard Reid Architects

Right: **Lower Mill Estate, Gloucestershire, UK.** Sundance Villa by Richard Reid. Inspired by the Californian Case Study Houses, this design turns and opens to the sun

Below: **Lower Mill Estate, Gloucestershire, UK.** Private House by Eva Jiricna, designed to maximise the pleasure of living in a nature reserve, whatever the weather

Right and below: **Lower Mill Estate, Gloucestershire, UK.** Deck-Spec House by Roger Sherman is designed to recall a dock, with moored boats which can slide out into the water to reveal different leisure opportunities below – such as a hot tub and lap pool. A giant canvas umbrella can unfold on top to provide outdoor shelter from rain or sun

Above and right: **Lower Mill Estate, Gloucestershire, UK.** The Boat House by Sutherland Hussey Architects, another variation on the boathouse motif, with real mooring space below a large outdoor room, and composed of various volumes within an overall structure clad with timber slats

Left and below: **Lower Mill Estate, Gloucestershire, UK.** Orchid House by Sarah Featherstone. Taking inspiration from the Bee Orchid that grows locally, this house is designed to melt into the background, its organic shapes offering flexible accommodation around the kitchen at its heart

Above and right: **Lower Mill Estate, Gloucestershire, UK.** Watermark House by Piers Gough of CZWG. Reached by boat or bridge, this spiralling house takes its inhabitants on a journey, via its staircase, past a first floor of conventional bedrooms, to an open-plan kitchen/living room with its own terrace on the second floor, before culminating in a roof space whose shape implies infinity and which offers a terrace and swimming pool under the stars

The Architects

Nigel Anderson of Robert Adam Architects

London - and Winchester - based Robert Adam Architects has a reputation for combining tradition with the latest technology in classical and traditional architecture and design. Projects include town and country houses, residential developments, urban masterplans, commercial and public buildings in Britain, continental Europe, the Middle East, Japan, and the USA. Nigel Anderson graduated in 1982 from the Bartlett School of Architecture, University College London. He joined Robert Adam Architects in 1988. His expertise covers a variety of areas including the restoration and refurbishment of historic houses, high-quality housing, urban developments and commercial work.

Archistudio

Tomasz Studniarek and Malgorzata Pilinkiewicz are the principals of the Katowice, Poland-based architecture practice, Archistudio, established in 1992. They both studied architecture at Silesian Technical University, Gliwice and graduated in 1990, after which they worked together at an architecture studio in the Netherlands. Their completed buildings have a wide range – civic works such as the District Courts of Justice, Katowice; educational works with the Rector's House at the Academy of Economics, Katowice; industrial warehouses; retail shops; restaurants and pubs; and residential works. Several of their completed projects have won awards and their work is widely featured in magazines and books.

Audrey Matlock Architect

Audrey Matlock Architect is based in Manhattan. Glass and steel is a recurring motif in their work. In addition to residential design, the company also specialises in urban design and masterplanning and innovative public projects including libraries, exhibition spaces, hotels, theatres and offices. A new building for the New York Aquarium is an example of the company's public work. Renovation is also a specialism, for instance schools and retail. One of Audrey Matlock Architect's new designs, a corporate headquarters for Armstrong World Industries in Virginia received the American Institute of Architects Award for Excellence.

Baumschlager & Eberle

Carlo Baumschlager and Dietmar Eberle founded their partnership in 1985. The company now has offices in Austria, Liechtenstein, Switzerland and China. Their work is modern with clean sleek lines, unadorned exteriors and light airy interiors, sustainable and energy-efficient whether private and public housing, commercial, or public buildings. Baumschlager & Eberle has won numerous local and international awards, and one of their residential designs, the innovative Lohbach development in Innsbruck won amongst other honours the Mies van der Rohe Award, EU Prize for Contemporary Architecture, and World Architecture Award for Housing Design and Sustainable Design.

Mikael Bergquist

Architect Mikael Bergquist studied at KTH, Stockholm and Academy of Fine Arts, Copenhagen. He established his own studio in Stockholm in 1996. Design projects include the Design Museum, Stockholm; Haga Park Museum and Café, Stockholm; The Copper Tents, Stockholm; Slefringe Renovation and Poolhouse extension (this won the Östergötlands Architectural Prize, 2004); Art Exhibition Hall, Kalmar; and Visitor Centre, Royal Castle and Park, Drottningholm (2005 – 06). Mikael Bergquist has lectured at several schools of architecture in Sweden, and curated a number of exhibitions. His latest book is *Accidentism: Josef Frank* published by Birkhäuser, 2005.

Derick de Bruyn

South African born Derick de Bruyn studied architecture at the University of Natal, Durban, and Kingston University, London. He worked in practices in South Africa, London, Milan and The Hague before establishing Derick de Bruyn Architects in 1996, in South Africa. Selected South African work includes House Pula in Centurion that received a Pretoria Institute for Architecture Merit Award for Outstanding Architecture and a Dulux Colour Award. The design for House Mabet in Tshwane received a South African Institute for Architects National Merit Award for Excellence in 1997. His work has been published in several interior magazines such as *House & Leisure and Elle Decoration*.

Eric Parry Architects

Eric Parry founded his London-based practice in 1983. The company also has an office in Kuala Lumpur. Eric Parry Architects' diverse range of projects includes artists' studios for Antony Gormley and Tom Phillips, in London; bars at the Ministry of Sound nightclub, in London; Damai Suria Apartments in Kuala Lumpur; the Mandarin Oriental Hyde Park Hotel Spa, in London; a number of office buildings in London's financial district; and Pembroke College, Cambridge University which won numerous awards. Urban planning is a major aspect of the company's work. Eric Parry is a former President of the Architectural Association and has lectured at Cambridge and Harvard Universities and Tokyo Institute of Technology.

Fearon Hay

Fearon Hay is an Auckland-based practice founded in 1998 and comprised of Jeff Fearon and Tim Hay. They graduated from the University of Queensland and University of Auckland respectively in the mid-1990s. Fearon Hay specialises in residential architecture in diverse environments – urban, coastal, lakeside, alpine – and inspiration comes from the surrounding countryside. A majority of the company's work is in New Zealand but it also has clients in Australia and the USA. Stylistically designs are modern, minimal and light with a distinct connection with the immediate landscape. Fearon Hay offers a complete package of building design, interiors and landscaping.

Sean Godsell Architects

Sean Godsell graduated from the University of Melbourne in 1984. After working in London, he returned to Melbourne and formed Godsell Associates Architects in 1994. His work has won many awards including a World Architecture Award 2001 (Best Building of the Region for the Carter/Tucker house) and AIA Architectural Record Award of Excellence 2003 (for his Peninsula House). Sean Godsell's designs have been published in international architectural journals including *Architectural Review* (UK), *Architectural Record* (USA), *Domus* (Italy) and *A+U* (Japan). In 2005 the magazine *Time* named him in the 'Who's Who' section of a 'Style and Design' supplement.

Timothy Hatton

Timothy Hatton studied Architecture at the University of Cambridge and at Harvard University Graduate School of Design. He has taught at Bartlett School of Architecture, University College London. After gaining experience with José Luis Sert in Boston and Colin St John Wilson in London, Timothy Hatton established his own London-based practice in 1985. The practice has worked on a number of commissions for residential housing, particularly refurbishments where the architects have overcome the constraints of working within the restrictions imposed by English Heritage listed status. One example of this is the eighteenth-century Stanley House, King's Road, London.

Steven Holl Architects

Steven Holl studied architecture at the University of Washington. In 1976 he formed his architecture practice in New York. Commissions include the Chapel of St Ignatius, Seattle University (1997); the Kiasma Museum of Contemporary Art, Helsinki (1998); the Cranbrook Institute of Science, Bloomfield Hills, Michigan (1998); Simmons Hall, Massachusetts Institute of Technology (2002); and Ralph Rapson Hall at the University of Minnesota (2002). His projects have been exhibited at the Museum of Modern Art, New York, Walker Art Centre, Minneapolis, and Henry Art Gallery, Seattle. In 2002, he received the National Design Award for Architecture from the Smithsonian Institution.

Marcio Kogan

Marcio Kogan graduated from Mackenzie School of Architecture, São Paulo in 1976. His professional work soon began to earn awards, for instance in 1983, the IAB award (Institute of Architects of Brazil) for the Rubens Sverner Day-Care Centre. His work covers a variety of structures such as residential houses, churches, museums and hotels and includes the Microbiology Museum and Fasano Hotel, both in São Paulo. His work has been exhibited in museums and at the IV Architecture Biennial of Brazil. His Du Plessis Residence, featured in this book, was awarded *Architectural Record* House of 2004.

Kengo Kuma & Associates

Kengo Kuma graduated from the School of Engineering at the University of Tokyo in 1979, followed by post-graduate studies at Columbia University, New York. In 1990 he founded Kengo Kuma & Associates. His aim is to "recover the tradition of Japanese buildings" with twenty-first-century interpretations. Kengo Kuma's recent work includes Nagasaki Prefecture Museum (2005); Fukusaki Hanging Garden (2005) and Shibuya Station (2003). He has won numerous awards, for instance the Architectural Institute of Japan Award, and his work has been exhibited in Japan and in Europe, including twice at the Venice Biennale.

Lacaton & Vassal

Lacaton & Vassal is an innovative architecture practice founded in 1987 and based in Bordeaux. It comprises Anne Lacaton and Jean-Philippe Vassal. Important works include the University of Grenoble and the Centre of Contemporary Creation at the Palais de Tokyo, Paris, and they are also well known for their residential housing projects. Their tendency to use new building materials not only keeps the cost down but also adds an avant-garde aspect to their work. Lacaton & Vassal won the World Architecture Award in 2001 and the 5th Prize for European Architecture by the Mies van der Rohe Foundation, 1997.

Leroy Street Studio

Leroy Street Studio, based in Manhattan, was founded in 1995 by Morgan Hare and Marc Turkel. They met whilst studying architecture at Yale University. Their designs for residential and commercial buildings can be seen in New York, several US states, and the British Isles. As well as creating high-end designs such as those for Bridge House, Long Island, and a Victorian Estate in England, the company is also dedicated to community architecture and design education. For this, Hester Street Collaborative was formed, a non-profit workshop, to initiate design/build projects in the community, working with local artists and students.

Qingyun Ma

Qingyun Ma is an architecture graduate from the University of Pennsylvania. In 1999 he founded the practice MADA s.p.a.m. in his native China and is very busy contributing to the modern Chinese urban landscape. His work includes residential and commercial developments in Qingpu (a fast-growing area of Shanghai) – specifically the innovative Thumb Island, a community centre that floats on a lake; and Qiao Zi Wan, a commercial district located on an oval-shaped piece of land surrounded by canals. Another of his major designs is the Ningbo Cultural Centre, a civic facility on the banks of the Yangtze River.

McAdam Architects

McAdam Architects was established by James McAdam and Tanya Kalinina in 1998. They worked together as directors at Alsop Architects in Moscow where they designed a number of major projects such as the award-winning Millennium House and Deutsche Bank CIS Headquarters. McAdam Architects has offices in London and Moscow and works on a wide range of buildings including public and cultural, retail and office developments, residential, and urban planning and regeneration. The house featured in this book was designed and managed by Tanya Kalinina, started briefly at Alsop Architects but developed and built with McAdam Architects.

Niall McLaughlin Architects

Niall McLaughlin was born in Geneva and educated at University College Dublin. He founded his own London-based practice in 1990 and it specialises in high-quality modern architecture with an inventive use of building materials, and commitment to the relationship between the building and its surroundings. In 1998 Niall McLaughlin was selected as UK Young Architect of the Year. His company has produced a wide range of work including the Arts Council, Exeter; Battery Park Subway, New York; and the Alzheimer's Centre, Dublin. In 2001 Niall McLaughlin was made honorary fellow of the Royal Institute of Architects in Ireland for achievements in architecture.

John Outram Associates

Established in 1973, John Outram Associates has a reputation for innovation, low-energy design, and an inventive use of traditional materials. The company was one of Britain's representatives at the 1991 Venice Architecture Biennale. Several of their works have won awards, including the Judge Institute of Management Studies, Cambridge University (1995), voted by townsfolk as 'the best building of the decade'; and a private house in Sussex (1989), considered by *The Sunday Times* newspaper as "the best house built in Britain since the war". Another prestigious project is an addition to the sixteenth-century Town Hall in the Groenmarkt, The Hague.

John Pardey Architects

John Pardey Architects was founded in 1988. It has twice been included in the Architecture Foundation/British Government Department of Culture, Media and Sport publication *New Architects* – a guide to Britain's best new practices. The practice has won numerous awards for housing, education, commercial and civic design. Work by John Pardey Architects has been widely featured in magazines, on television and in books. John Pardey is the author of *Utzon: Two houses on Majorca* (2005) – shortlisted for the RIBA Bookshops International Book of the Year Award; and *Beyond Louisiana: The Work of Vilhelm Wohlert* (2006).

Richard Reid & Associates

Richard Reid and Associates, based in Sevenoaks, Kent, work with buildings of a variety of scales from corner shop to city planning. The practice was appointed masterplanner for the district of Kleinzschocher, Leipzig, Germany (1995) and masterplanner and architect for The Lower Mill Estate, a development of 575 holiday houses set in a landscape of lakes in Gloucestershire. The practice is also creating, for the City of Bologna and the University of Bologna, the masterplan of a large site on the edge of the city, in association with Piero Sartogo of Sartogo Architetti Associati, Richard Meier & Partners, and Studio Arco..

Mack Scogin Merrill Elam Architects

Mack Scogin and Merrill Elam have worked together for over 30 years. The firm, based in Atlanta, Georgia, was founded in 1984. Their work is diverse – public and private buildings including residential, museums & galleries, libraries, government and civic. Amongst their projects are Pittsburgh Children's Museum; United States Courthouse, Austin, Texas; Arizona State Law Library; and Ohio State University School of Architecture, the latter winning the 2005 National American Institute of Architects (AIA) / ALA Award of Excellence. The Mountain Tree House, featured in this book, won the 2005 National AIA Honour Award of Excellence.

Eduardo Souto de Moura

Portuguese architect Eduardo Souto de Moura studied at the School of Fine Arts, Oporto, and was later appointed Professor in its Faculty of Architecture. His commissions range from private houses to sports stadiums. Recent projects include houses in Porto; the renovation of Braga's Municipal Market; a house and wine cellar in Valladolid, Spain; renovation of the Museu Grão Vasco at Viseu; the Museum of Transport and Communication, Oporto; several metro stations in Oporto; and (with Alvaro Siza) the Portuguese Pavilion, Expo 2000 in Hanover. His work has won several awards in Portugal.

John Winter

John Winter completed his studies at London's Architectural Association in 1953. He finished his first building, a house, in 1956, mentioned in Nikolaus Pevsner's book North-East Norfolk and Norwich (1962) from the Buildings of England series. He formed his own practice in 1964 and took on a diverse range of projects. Diversity has been a theme in his career: as well as designing buildings, he has taught at academic institutions throughout the world; written several books, including *Modern Architecture* published in 1969; exhibited work, for instance at New York's Museum of Modern Art; won numerous awards; and in 1984 received the MBE for services to architecture.

Cazú Zegers

Chilean architect Cazú Zegers studied at the Universidad Católica de Valparaíso and spent two years working in New York before establishing his Santiago-based practice in 1990. He has undertaken projects in industrial, commercial and residential architecture, furniture and lighting design, and urban planning, and has a particular interest in developing ideas based on the relationship between poetry and architecture and the application of cutting-edge technologies. His design for the Casa Cala, Lago Ranco (1993) won the Gran Premio Latinoamericano de Arquitectura at the Buenos Aires Bienal. In 1999 he founded the AIRA Workshop (Arte-Imaginación-Rigor-Amor) in collaboration with Juan Pablo Almarza, who graduated from the Universidad Católica de Valparaíso in 1996.